Who Moved My Servers?

WHO MOVED MY SERVERS?

How developing an agile cloud-first strategy will help you get ideas to your customers faster

NEIL MILLARD

RETHINK PRESS

First published in Great Britain in 2019 by Rethink Press
(www.rethinkpress.com)

Contents

SECTION 1

MAINFRAMES TO CLOUDS

Introduction

My idea of utopia is the choice to do what you want, when you want. By leveraging automation, I believe everything can be provided for in abundance. Food farmed or created. Housing everywhere. Work? Not really heard of. After all, if everyone has food and accommodation provided, most of your income is no longer needed.

Let's have fun, pursue true happiness and fulfilment. Play games, read books, study history or philosophy.

Maybe the robots can take over the world, and we can live in a zoo, where the robots feed us and allow us to do whatever we want and go wherever we want.

There are many dystopian views too, and as a positive person, I choose to focus on the utopian. If you want a taste of what this might look like, then I encourage you to put the Culture series of books by Iain M Banks on your reading list.

I have four steps to help us deliver this value. Design, automation, scaling and data.

Design is sometimes called a minimum viable product, and isn't the long and time-consuming step that it once was. Agile says we need to do just enough design to start delivering value.

Automation is where we build what we have designed, and perhaps revisit the design and build to improve the automation in an iterative way.

Scaling is where the biggest excitement and the biggest headaches of a product or start-up lay. Having a small perfectly formed pizza is good to start with, but not quite going to cut it if you want to feed an army of conference delegates in one sitting.

Data and keeping it safe is crucial. It's the most valuable thing we have as individuals other than our time.

Ensuring it doesn't get lost or stolen, either through hardware failure or theft, must be taken seriously.

Perhaps that is a bit deep for the first page of this book, so let me introduce myself.

ONE

whoami

These days I'm often described as a DevOps engineer, and it's been quite a journey from where I started out. My first love is programming, and it was my first experience with computers in the 80s. Programming basic games on a ZX Spectrum, then an Amiga using machine code.

At thirteen I moved to upper school and found some acceptance with four fellow geeks – a friendship circle that I still enjoy and am very grateful for today.

Working a paper-round allowed me to save up enough to buy a second-hand ZX Spectrum, and after that computer games and magazines. In these magazines you could find listings for computer programs and games. Yes, pages and pages of code to type in and save to cassette tape. While laborious, this process effectively taught me how others coded. All in ZX Spectrum BASIC, line by line, including lots of numbers that I didn't quite understand, but seemed to be related to graphics on the screen.

Before long I was teaching myself machine code for the Zilog Z80 CPU, and with the help of Romantic Robot's Multiface, I could decode (to some extent) the games I loved playing. With companies like Codemasters in their infancy, the dream was to create a game and retire on the proceeds.

I lost myself in computer programming – and listening to Kylie Minogue in my bedroom.

While I was working jobs at college, I became the proud owner of a Commodore Amiga A500, which meant I had traded up to programming the Motorola 68000 CPU with the luxury of floppy disks instead of tapes. I learned about everything I could. At this point that consisted of 3D graphics, the Amiga's Blitter chip affectionally called Fat Agnus and hardware level floppy disk routines.

While still at college I had learned about connecting computers across phone lines using modems. These devices allowed your computer to connect to another computer and exchange files, messages and read information. These host computers were known as Bulletin Board Systems (BBSs), and were usually run by hobbyists as a way of connecting communities of like-minded geeks together. As only one person could connect at a time, the more popular BBSs would not let you connect unless you had the latest modems running at the fastest connection speeds.

The BBSs I connected to provided more computer code to look through, as well as contributed to the community by sharing mine in the way of producing computer demos. These small programs would look like short videos of colours, patterns, graphics, music and most important, the scroller. The scroller is a continuous line of text making up sentences which you would read while watching the contortions of shapes and colour bouncing around to the music.

This gave me a sense of belonging and community, and introduced me to a few good eggs that encouraged my programming journey.

When I finished college, I bought an Amiga 2000, the much larger cousin of the A500. I used this to set up my own BBS, which was great as the files and code would then come to me, rather than the long hours required to connect and download from the other BBSs. However, this being 1994, the internet was about to make itself known. FidoNet, unlike most BBSs using a hub and spoke system, used a store and forward system. In this way, a network of servers would connect to each other on demand or on a schedule. This was a much more efficient way of sharing information, and gave access to some of UseNet, another very popular forum and messaging platform.

This system also enabled emails. You could create an email, upload it to your nearest FidoNet node, and the network would do the rest. With dialup access to the internet, the BBS was becoming endangered, as was the Amiga as my chosen platform. It wouldn't be long before I was hosting websites and email servers on the internet instead.

In 1995 I got the chance to start my IT career as a trainee technician. Rather than joining as a programmer, I secured a job as a trainee. This was on the hardware track and not the software track as I had dreamed. My focus turned to hardware: IBM compatible PCs and EPoS shop checkouts. Most of my day was spent driving parts around the beautiful West Country. This was broken up with short bursts of installing, replacing and in some cases repairing tills with a soldering iron.

As a trainee, I was taught about printers, hard drives, replacing power supplies and later about installing software to new computers in the offices of Railtrack and Wessex Water. After two years I graduated from trainee status to technician, together with a nice raise and a new company car.

During the next two years my understanding of client operating systems grew, moving from DOS 6 to Windows 95 and even Windows NT 4. I learned a great deal about networking, TCP/IP, Token Ring, Ethernet, and structured cabling, sometimes called CAT5. However, I was frustrated that I couldn't get involved with setting up servers, and the thought of programming was never far from my mind.

After a few years in desktop support, I was experienced enough to move on to configuring and supporting servers. The traditional infrastructure role, looking after physical servers in a data centre, together with all the bits that hold it together: networks, storage arrays, Fibre, etc.

Then Sanctuary Housing invited me to join their infrastructure team.

The IT department was in three groups: the helpdesk, business application support, and infrastructure. During my six years at Sanctuary, I would spend time in all three, but at the start I was in the infrastructure team. The infrastructure team was further split into four teams: network, client, security and server. I had the title of Server Technician.

As I arrived on the first day, there was a chair, a desk and a box. My first job was to build my desktop PC that was to serve me for the next two years. This was a slightly automated affair once I'd plugged it in, as there was already a PXE server to load Windows and the standard software. My next challenge was to build a Citrix server. At Sanctuary Housing, most IT users not in head office accessed the systems via Wyse Terminal connected to a Citrix server. This put a never-ending demand on new Citrix servers as the company grew in turnover and staff.

Citrix server number forty-seven. That was what I was building. Another team member that started a week later than I did was building server forty-eight. This first build was interesting, but boring and repetitive after the third or fourth time. Given this was one of the main activities initially, it was a lot of time spent on a process that had so many manual steps. As time grew, we refined the process so that it was easy to build Citrix servers, often ten at a time. Blade technology was coming into its own, and HP provided a chassis that could house sixteen quad processor servers. Each of these would have the Xen Hypervisor installed to enable virtual servers to run on it, and this in turn would host about ten Citrix servers. To build these manually would have taken a lot of time and resulted in many mistakes. Automation of this process was key to support the growth of the organisation.

Within the Microsoft world, there are a suite of products under the banner of System Center. This started off with Configuration Manager, which is a configuration management system. The equivalent in the UNIX or Linux space is Puppet or Chef. Configuration management enables you to build and deploy computer systems from a single console. This includes building the computer right through to installing software and keeping that software updated with the desired versions of programs.

The System Center suite had the addition of Microsoft Operations Manager, commonly called MOM.

This system allows rules to run against your managed machines (mostly servers), to check the status and performance of the applications, including the machine they run on. Should the system break any rules or breach a performance threshold, alerts are raised to inform support personnel that the server needs attention.

At the heart of the design of SCOM (System Center Operations Manager) vs. MOM is the concept of a monitor and rollups to create the overview of a whole system. These aggregate monitors enable the creation of a dashboard to show the overall status of many systems with end-to-end monitors, including the status of degraded. A degraded service is one that is still able to operate, but is experiencing some level of failure that will reduce performance or redundancy. The next evolution in this automation, after build and monitor, is to design the reaction and response when an alert is triggered. This reduces support tasks through automating the recovery of failed service components. In the SCOM literature this is called Diagnostic and Recovery. Two tasks are defined as part of the monitor (or alert): upon the alert trigger from the monitor, the diagnostic task is run – each diagnostic task can then execute a recovery step, such as restarting a service if the diagnostic reports that it has stopped.

With the systems becoming more automated, I was able to focus on other work. A project I particularly enjoyed was the helpdesk software upgrade. Most businesses run processes (whether formally written down or not) and most call centres deal with a lot of enquiries – and a busy IT service desk is no exception. Working with IT management to understand what and why certain processes exist helped me work with the software provider to install and set up the new service desk software. Part of the vision was to streamline some tasks and automate others.

Taking my experience of automating server-side recovery tasks, it was useful to apply these lessons to create a self-service portal for the IT customers and users. In this way, some of the simpler orders could be requested directly by the customer, and the automated provisioning systems would then provide and action the required steps to deliver the product or service the customer had ordered. This was first available to IT staff for ordering such things as software installs, access to software via Citrix, and even the provisioning of a VDI (Virtual Desktop Infrastructure) machine to use. This created great consoles and customer experiences easily demonstrated by the Amazon Web Services™ Console.

Because of these achievements I was promoted to senior technician, and later, support team leader. Unfortunately, this latest promotion took me away from the creative tasks I love, so I filled a great deal of my spare time looking for a programming project.

My programming had taken a back seat for long enough. I was just starting to implement automated responses to server alerts, allowing the servers themselves to tell you that something needs attention. This was stimulating my programming juices, and around 2012 I started to hear about something called DevOps. It was sold to me as infrastructure guys writing programs to fix faults spotted by the monitoring and alerting systems.

Meanwhile, programming had developed in the marketplace. I was never trained as a programmer beyond A Levels, but terms like SCRUM and Agile seemed to go hand in hand with DevOps. My career made a slight pivot, and now I can share my learnings with you.

An individual with a DevOps title in the IT profession will tell you there is no such thing as a DevOps engineer when used to describe their job. DevOps is better described as a business function, where a team with differing skills and experiences work together to facilitate the delivery of IT products and services.

To get the best performance, this team must consist of someone to understand the product, someone to develop the solution, someone to test it, and someone to ensure it delivers. SCRUM and Agile frameworks have good labels for these team members, and I will describe them further in the chapter about key concepts.

A transformation project, as cloud and Agile migration projects are often called, are much more than just DevOps. As well as the team mentioned earlier, the management needs to be on board and understand the new ways of working, as well as the practices in place to provide a view on planning, progression and completeness of the project(s).

The next section will cover what the cloud is, what it means, and how you and your business can benefit from it. I will cover the joy of throw-away virtual machines, the available cloud providers such as Amazon Web Services and Google, and share my thoughts about hybrid solutions offered by VMWare™, Pivotal and Data Centres.

The cloud and Agile practices are not without their problems of course. I will share my DevOps knowledge about working with customers on transformation projects and the problems they came up against, as well as the solutions. There are also technical problems moving applications and services to the cloud, and these will be addressed also.

Finally, I will cover the steps required to implement cloud infrastructure and project delivery, so you can journey boldly and confidently to help your project or company embrace the cloud, save money and deliver a great experience to your customers.

And just maybe we can automate ourselves to utopia.

TWO

What Is Cloud?

Someone or something (in the case of automated processes) will provide a service and look after some aspects of running that service. These are classified into three levels:

1. **IaaS:** Infrastructure as a service. This is at the basic level like Amazon Web Services EC2 (IaaS) that provides a server attached to a network. The configuration and running of that server is up to you.

2. **PaaS:** Platform as a service. More aspects of the platform are supported by your provider. Examples are Heroku™ for application hosting.

3. **SaaS:** Software as a service. At this advanced level such as Shopify™, Xero™ or Expensify™ you request the service and they look after the code, servers, etc.

The National Institute of Standards and Technology (NIST) published a definition of cloud computing[1] in September 2011:

> Cloud computing is a model for enabling convenient, on-demand network access to a shared pool of configurable computing resources (e.g., networks, servers, storage, applications, and services) that can be rapidly provisioned and released with minimal management effort or service provider interaction. This Cloud model promotes availability and is composed of five essential characteristics (On-demand self-service, Broad network access, Resource pooling, Rapid elasticity, Measured Service); three service models (Cloud Software as a Service (SaaS), Cloud Platform as a Service (PaaS), Cloud Infrastructure as a Service (IaaS)); and, four deployment models

---

1 P. Mell and T. Grance (2011) *The Nist Definition of Cloud Computing*. Gaithersburg, MD: National Institute of Standards and Technology, available at https://csrc.nist.gov/publications/detail/sp/800-145/final

(Private Cloud, Community Cloud, Public Cloud, Hybrid Cloud). Key enabling technologies include: (1) fast wide-area networks, (2) powerful, inexpensive server computers, and (3) high-performance virtualisation for commodity hardware.

Of the five essential characteristics, On-demand self-service, Rapid elasticity and Measured service are worth going into more detail.

On-demand self-service

This is where a consumer can provision computing capabilities automatically, without requiring human interaction. This level of automation enables fast and accurate provisioning of computing power including associated services, such as network storage, whenever your application needs it. This can be delivered in two ways:

- **Rapid elasticity:** The appearance of unlimited resources that can be elastically provisioned and released, in some cases automatically, to scale rapidly outward and inward to match demand.

- **Measured service:** Automatically controlling and optimising resource use, for example by using a metering capability for by-the-minute billing. Resource usage can be monitored, controlled and reported, providing transparency for the provider and consumer of utilised services.

Let's contrast this with the five stages of computer evolution:

1. Mainframes provided a central resource accessed by computer terminals. Access was limited to CPU cycles or time on the mainframe required to run your programs and processes in a private session.
2. During the 1980s, home computers became widely available, with computing resources available for private stand-alone usage.
3. During the 1990s, businesses increased their use of computers outside of the finance department. The need to share information and the rise of Microsoft Windows saw data servers introduced into individual offices and shared among the computers.

4. Into the 2000s, the commoditisation of server hardware (blades) gave rise to private Data Centres and further optimised using virtualisation.

5. The rise of virtual infrastructure enabled cloud providers selling compute time by the minute from public multi-tenant data centres.

As a child of the 80s (I was born in 1975) I have first-hand experience of all these stages.

I acquired much of my server knowledge during the 2000s, when I worked for Sanctuary Housing. Their computing model was not dissimilar to the mainframes where a pool of Citrix servers, a type of Windows server that could share private desktop sessions, were accessed using remote terminals consisting of a screen, keyboard, mouse and network connection.

As the company was growing rapidly, the server team and I had the task of providing an ever-growing resource of Citrix servers, while the desktop team ran flat out setting up and shipping terminals to all the new offices.

Running your own data centre has many pros and cons. The rapid elasticity is backed by a team of server technicians buying, building and installing the ever-growing number of servers. For a business this is a capital expense.

This process takes time, usually weeks. First comes the business process of buying the server hardware, then the lead time for the supplier to deliver the servers. Once received, the servers need building. The components such as CPU and memory are shipped separately and need to be installed into the servers. Assuming sufficient capacity in the data centre, both in terms of physical space and cooling and power, the servers are installed into racks within the data centre, ready for the next step of installing software and configuration.

The latter step was mostly automated, as the server can run programs and set itself up according to the configuration supplied to the new server. This step is also required when provisioning IaaS servers.

Moving the provisioning to server blades (smaller servers optimised for data centres) and later using Xen virtualisation, the provisioning time reduced per server as they were virtualised with many sharing bigger hardware servers, enabling batch setups.

When you request a server in the cloud, with the exception of the server setup, all the steps are done for you and the lead time for the virtual server is measured in seconds. This frees up a huge amount of setup time, both in the sense of delivery and lead time of the servers (hardware), and the engineering time to physically install and set them up.

To facilitate and manage virtual servers, the public cloud providers enable you to purchase virtual servers on a pay-as-you-go basis. They also manage the infrastructure, data centres, network, etc, which removes a lot of the admin and setup overhead.

Rapid elasticity

A major part of the cloud definition is On-demand and Elasticity. Usually the cloud provider, both private and public, will enable the request for new servers via a web interface or Application Program Interface (API). Together with access controls and audit records, this enables authorised users to spin up a cloud server in seconds.

This action equates to switching on a brand-new server. I'm sure you recall the last time you received a new computer or laptop. It usually came with a pre-installed operating system, but then you had to spend the next few minutes or hours (or days in some cases), setting it up to your liking and installing software so it was usable. The same is true of the cloud server: spinning it up is just like switching on that brand-new computer.

Part of the role of DevOps is to put processes and automation in place so that after spinning up the server, it configures itself, ready for work in a few minutes. The main reason for this is that cloud providers use cheap commodity hardware. The main cost of running the server is the electricity, not the hardware itself.

This is not the same hardware you would often find in an onsite data centre. What I'm referring to is the concept of a server that is not designed to be switched off, ever. The sort of server where most, if not all, the components can be swapped out in the event of a failure, while the server is still operating. No, the server hardware in the cloud is not like that: it's cheap and does its job just fine. The thing to remember is that it will eventually fail.

This means the systems running on and with the server must expect failure and be able to cope with it. Anyone can spin up a server in the cloud, but a DevOps team of developers and system operators can write code so that the server is running in less than ten minutes. It can do this repeatedly and reliably, so when the server does fail, the impact to your application is a small degradation in service, while the systems seamlessly build you a new one.

Measured service

With the ability to create servers at the click of a button or by using automation, reacting to a large demand on the servers, without adequate monitoring, could leave you with a large bill.

The cloud provider will provide measuring in several forms. These are based on how many servers have been requested and delivered, how many are running at any given time, the run time of those servers, together with the cost and billing.

In addition to the resource and billing side of things, the servers are also monitored from a health and performance perspective. Is the server still responding to the hypervisor – can the physical server still see the virtual server it is hosting? Can the network hear the server normally?

In addition to these basic checks, monitoring also includes CPU and network usage and sometimes memory usage. With the automation of server configuration, together with monitoring CPU and network usage, thresholds can be set to enable the elastic growth of a load-balanced application to scale out.

In addition to the basic monitoring offered by the cloud provider, you'll want further monitoring so you can check on the health of not only the server or servers (in a cluster), but the health of the application or services to your customers. More of this will be covered in the next chapter.

If you are still hesitant about using cloud, you're not alone. The most common issues are security and data storage. Specifically, whether you can store your data where it won't be lost or stolen.

This was a big issue in 2008, but with newer services, such as Amazon Web Services' VPC (Virtual Private Cloud), private networks with a link to your offices, and no inbound internet access, there's a much smaller attack area and thus improved security.

Of the public cloud providers, AWS certainly has the lead both in products available and customers served.

With over 50% of the potential market not using cloud, and a fraction of that just using it for development purposes, there is a long way to go in terms of growth.

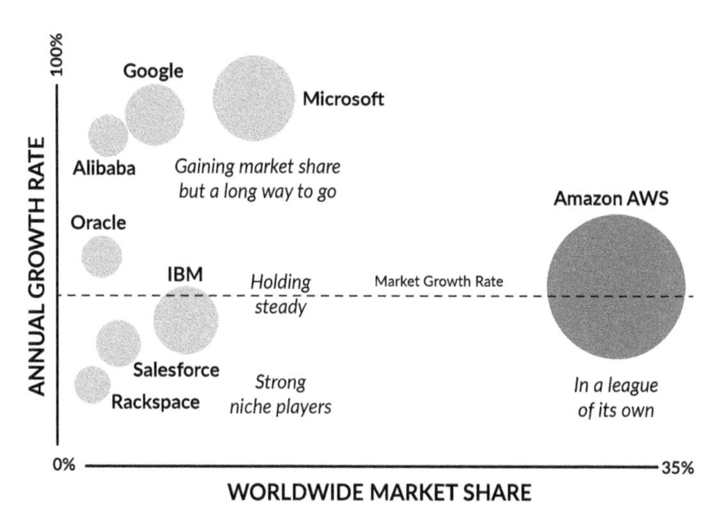

***Figure 2.1**: Cloud provider market share statistics. © Synergy Research Group 2018, https://www.srgresearch.com/articles/cloud-market-keeps-growing-over-40-amazon-still-increases-share*

The major players are still growing at over 50% per year with AWS growing and holding its market share lead. Synergy estimates that cloud infrastructure revenues are in excess of $48 billion per year, and growing at well over 40% per year.

THREE

What Is DevOps?

There are developers who care about production and server infrastructure. There are Sysops and infrastructure technicians who can develop programs. But there's still a gap between these two specialists. DevOps is where these two resources work together, teaching each other about testing, deployments, monitoring and performance. More recently it has come to define those with infrastructure and development experience, having already learned through experience. I'm an infrastructure person first, but have always had an understanding of programming.

The term 'DevOps' was first coined in 2008 at the Agile conference, where agile infrastructure was discussed by Andrew Clay Shafer and Patrick Debois. It quite literally refers to developers using Agile methodologies to communicate and collaborate with server and network infrastructure professionals. This brings the slow and somewhat static world of infrastructure into the dynamic and fast-paced world of software development through automation and delivery using both tools and culture.

The term Agile was first coined for this in 2001, in the Manifesto for Agile Software Development (Agile Manifesto) where a group of seventeen software developers came together in Utah to discuss lightweight software development methods. Its roots are a bit older and stem from ideas in the 1990s, such as rapid application development, scrum and feature-driven development to name a few.

The Agile Manifesto is based on twelve principles:[2]

1. Customer satisfaction by early and continuous delivery of valuable software
2. Welcoming changing requirements, even in late development

---

2 Kent Beck et al (2001), http://agilemanifesto.org/principles.html

3. Working software delivered frequently (weeks rather than months)

4. Close, daily cooperation between business people and developers

5. Projects are built around motivated individuals, who should be trusted

6. Face-to-face conversation is the best form of communication (co-location)

7. Working software is the principal measure of progress

8. Sustainable development, able to maintain a constant pace

9. Continuous attention to technical excellence and good design

10. Simplicity – the art of maximising the amount of work not done – is essential

11. The best architectures, requirements and designs emerge from self-organising teams

12. The team regularly reflects on how to become more effective, and adjusts accordingly

To enable these ideas to propagate and enhance uptake, there have been further enhancements and evolutions for a spread of tools and frameworks. Most promote teamwork, collaboration and process adaptability throughout the product development lifecycle. In organisations with an agile culture you will see four primary processes:

Iterative

This process centres around small progressive evolutionary and incremental steps. Each iteration is timeboxed within a short period, often days or weeks, where a cross-functional team will discuss, design, create and test a new feature or bug fix with a working piece of software at the end of the timebox. It might not be enough to warrant a release or new version of the software, but it's a fully working part of the next release. Often at the beginning of a green project, where nothing exists, many of the initial tasks are one-off productions of scaffolding. At a new start-up for instance, this could consist of the creation of a cloud computing account and definition of networks, together with infrastructure service providing scheduling and build facilities. With an established team or company, a framework of the end-to-end service may be designed, with minimal aspects to each process in the service created during the first iteration.

Communication

In addition to team members working together closely, the product owner is present to provide answers to any questions posed by the team while they're developing, and provide guidance to ensure the return on time and money invested is maximised. Communication about the status of the project is shared by way of a publicly displayed information radiator or Kanban board. Should the team have outside dependencies, communication extends to them also. Bringing in expertise to the team as required, or team members working with other teams, will also help spread the vision and reduce the impact of blockers or impediments.

Adaptation

A very short feedback cycle is backed up by a daily stand-up meeting sometimes called the daily scrum. Team members will share their progress from the previous day, what they intend to complete today, and any impediments that may slow progress. Sharing progress in this way allows greater cooperation and for knowledge to be used across the team.

Quality

Continuous integration, test-driven development and pair programming help to improve product quality and enhance development agility.

It should be noted that it's too easy to be drawn into trying to be Agile without actually being agile. The framework and process are a proxy for delivery of value with fast feedback loops, supporting continuous improvement and delivery. I see many companies getting into the trap of renaming roles and processes to tick the Agile box, but without the fundamentals or having a clear understanding of impact on the day-to-day workings of product development.

Agile doesn't mean changes for the sake of change: there are still planning and deployment cycles so the teams know where they are heading. However, without some forethought, costs can be significantly different based on decisions in the design stage. Design tweaks can make a significant difference to AWS spend and therefore eat into the savings you thought you were going to provide.

During an iterative development, design is required to ensure certain non-functional requirements are still met. I have often seen that killer new feature implemented, but at the cost of limiting the ability of the application to grow. The resulting technical debt lurks until the inevitable scaling of the application is needed as the customer base and popularity grow.

The main drawback of Agile is where it fails to include operations early enough in the development cycle. DevOps adds to Agile by emphasising effective collaboration and cooperation across the entire IT department through extended teams to deliver software and a single, unified activity. From creating the software to delivering a return to the company, and ultimately through to the end user experience.

DevOps is a working culture that delivers software to its users with an optimised cycle of creation, test and delivery, resulting in a quicker return on investment and shorter time between failures.

There are several key voices leading the way in DevOps; Damon Edwards, John Willis and Jez Humble coined the acronym CALMS: Culture, Automation, Lean, Measurement and Sharing. Patrick Debois added to this, stating that DevOps is a human problem.

Culture is closely linked to behaviours and is certainly key when developing DevOps practices for your team. Getting this right isn't easy, but it's very important as it weaves throughout the behaviours of everyone involved.

Automation of processes is a great way to remove errors through repetitive cycles of work, allowing the team to engage their more creative side.

Lean is a nod to the Japanese manufacturing movement of the 80s and 90s where continuous improvement and reduction of waste provided a lean production process and reduced costs. This means focusing on where the value is and deferring anything else. Some planning and code are required, but just enough to be viable.

Measurement helps identify where bottlenecks and waste (two ends of the same scale) occur in systems, allowing further improvements to be made.

Sharing feeds back into the culture and feedback mechanisms, allowing the whole DevOps and CALMS movement to advance forward one iteration at a time.

Gene Kim has continued the pioneering research started by Patrick Debois in DevOps practices. Using Gene's interests in security operations, ITIL (Information Technology Infrastructure Library) created by the UK Government, and high-performing IT organisations, he has written several books on the subject, including his very successful book *The Phoenix Project*.

This book describes the journey of a manager dropped into a senior IT position following the dismissal of the previous guy, and shows by example how DevOps culture and practices can be introduced and embedded within an organisation, bringing together operations, application development, security and testing, improving effectiveness and efficiencies in the organisation.

DevOps teams

Team and inter-team organisation are big subjects. Suggested reading includes https://skeltonthatcher.com and works about Conway's Law.

The best functioning teams should be set up to remove or reduce the number of external dependencies either through individual team membership from a squad, or self-service of products from the provider team. Spotify wrote a white paper on their experiences, published in 2012, and coined squads and tribes as a way of describing a matrix team structure.

As Spotify is a company with a fail fast and learn culture, this view has evolved over time, together with the advances in automation, to provide autonomy and self-service in place of team meetings and cooperation.

This gives us two modes of engagement that a team can take with DevOps:

1. DevOps is advanced enough to provide a PaaS, and therefore the team and developers can self-serve any resources they require
2. A DevOps squad member joins the team helping the developer team, therefore internalising external dependencies

DevOps teams, sometimes called cross-functional teams or squads, are like the A Team in the IT world. Three to nine people that have every skill they need to design, create, test, deploy and deliver a solution to the customer. This includes operations and infrastructure, business analysts, developer and programmers, security, designers, database administrators, product owners, and any other skill the team needs for the project they are assigned. The resulting team has all the skills and access required to deliver a complete solution without external dependencies. These teams can work on one project at a time, and continue to work together on many projects depending on the scope of the work and customer.

Following SCRUM or Kanban processes and the principles of DevOps and Agile, the team works together to define, prioritise and estimate these tasks. The product owner works with the business analyst to create a list of items that will create value for the product owner. These may be new features, upgrades, defect fixes and other work. This is added to the backlog. The team is self-organising and breaks the project down into concrete tasks or steps, estimates the size of the tasks, and these are also added to the backlog. There may be a few iterations between the team estimation and the product owner, who is there to direct the tasks in order of importance or priority.

Figure 3.1 shows a workflow that involves all the roles in a lean team. A person in the team can take on one or more of these roles, depending on the size of team and the skills they have.

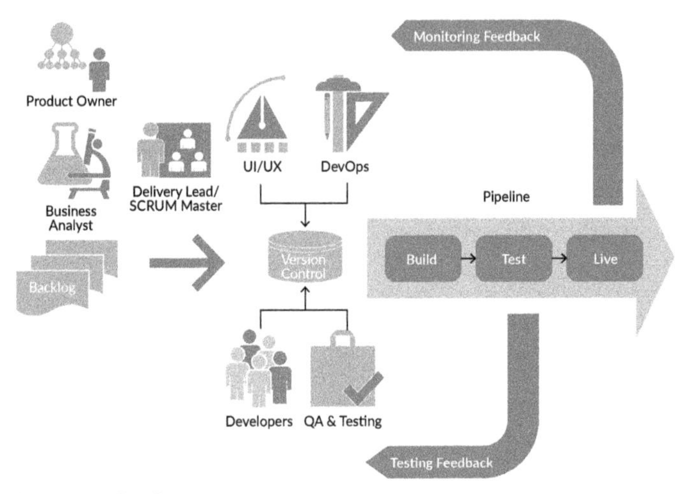

Figure 3.1: *A DevOps team*

There are more feedback loops than on this diagram, for instance UI and UX will get design and usability feedback from the user group or product owner.

Product owner role

This is the ultimate authority on the deliverables, and can be a stakeholder, budget holder or Subject Matter Expert (SME). They understand the business and the problem that it's experiencing, and how this project or product is going to help. They need to have knowledge of the product area and have some budget authority.

Business analyst role

A key role that acts in some sense as a design authority and sometimes a translator. Working with the product owner to understand the key outcomes and understanding the business processes that must be understood, followed or replaced by the application developed by the team.

Delivery lead/SCRUM master role

This role is often seen as a facilitator. They will coordinate planning and retrospective sessions, as well as liaising with other teams to resolve blockers and other issues hampering progress.

UI/UX role

The focus for this role is what the end user sees: usability of the software. This is an important early role that may work with the business analyst. From the initial user feedback and framework designs, to designing visuals and graphics, this role is focused on understanding the user experience, defining and shaping how the software looks, and how the processes are presented to the user. Usability is essential, as is getting user feedback and ideas about the software the team is developing. This feedback loop will ensure the developing product is fit for purpose and easy to use.

Developer role

This role writes tests and the functional code for the end software or product. They are an expert programmer and often have other skills that are classed in the other roles. The focus of this role is to create features, and sometimes tools. As bugs do appear, writing tests helps get fast feedback to reduce the bugs before deployment.

Quality assurance and testing role

The focus of this role is to ensure the software delivers the functionality specified by each task, without breaking anything else. As an expert in the area of testing, they will be writing and executing tests, or in some cases conducting manual tests themselves.

DevOps role

This role is responsible for delivering the tools and servers required by the DevOps team. The toolset of a DevOps team includes source control systems and continuous integration server(s).

Infrastructure and servers for development, and testing and production (live) environments, are built using automation and pipelines. They are also built with service monitoring to provide feedback to the team for reliability, scalability and performance.

Using the same continuous integration scheduling system, pipelines are created by DevOps or the team to build and test the code as progress is made.

All this is provided with as much self-service and automation as possible.

Other SMEs should be brought into the team when specific skills are needed. Examples include database administrators (DBAs), infrastructure architects, business users or other experts.

Once these resources are in the team, pair programming (where two team members work together on a task) is encouraged to enable the sharing of experience and knowledge among the team, thus decreasing the silos of information.

I have found that having a team member on loan for several specific tasks not only enables the knowledge of the team to grow, but the task to be achieved faster and with higher quality.

These loans provide many other benefits outside of the completion of tasks, including greater team cooperation and social ideas with chance conversations and wider social interactions.

SECTION 2

WHY CLOUD?

FOUR

Cloud Infrastructure Solutions

Traditional approaches to application design and deployment could leave you with downtime just when your customers want to spend money with you, or when you want to update the production service with that killer feature you and your team have been working on.

You may have heard about the success of start-ups moving fast and using the best of cloud technologies. Then why, you wonder, when you move away from one monolithic application to the cloud, do you see your downtime figure moving in the wrong direction?

While moving to the cloud means you no longer need a dedicated team of engineers for security updates, feature updates and bug fixes, it could lead to a sprawling mess of servers with data everywhere. How do you keep your cloud servers manageable and your data safe?

There are already tried-and-tested methods to migrate, re-platform and move towards customer-first, mobile-first and cloud-first applications – where you will save time, money and energy – and most important of all, keep the service running with little downtime and unsociable call-outs.

By using DevOps practices which blend the creation, testing and rigour of programming best practices, together with the practicalities of building and operating enterprise infrastructure environments, we build a cloud-first, Agile system. By utilising open source software with a plan, we create great results!

Application designed for cloud

To fully embrace the benefits of cloud, your application needs to be designed with an understanding of what the cloud can do for the application. The classic belief of one big application able to do anything and take weeks or even months to upgrade due to its monolithic structure is very outdated, and not useful to take advantage of cloud technologies.

I will cover the Agile development principles and microservices, both aimed at getting value to your customers as quickly as possible.

Automated infrastructure

DevOps is the result of developers and operations staff working together. Building servers or applications, creating tools, and self-service are the hallmarks of successful cloud-oriented teams. The keys to increasing efficiency of delivery is in the repetitive nature of build, test, deploy. Automating this makes it easier to get fast feedback for fast deployment, delivering value quicker. Having developers and operations staff work together also reduces friction involved in deployment and operations, allowing some organisations to release a new version of their software multiple times per hour. Without automation the process would simply be too slow, and the risk of errors would be great.

Scaling for flexible workloads

With the code deployment and infrastructure automated, flexibility and scale are possible for the servers providing the service to your customers. Scaling up to demand is as important as scaling down once the peak has past. This enables your business to spend the least on cloud infrastructure, while being able to deliver the most when your customers need it.

Keeping the data safe

With automation, data is moving around quickly with servers existing for a short time to meet demand, then disappearing. Care must be taken to ensure data is not lost in this process. In the early days at Google, they would log searches on the website, but this data wasn't seen as important, and would quickly become overwritten by other requirements. Of course, this is very different now, as that information is now a service in its own right (Google Analytics).

Cloud workloads

The value of setting up or moving to the cloud should be understood before planning anything. Ask yourself the following questions to help the planning process.

1. Does your company have and own a data centre?

This might not be an obvious place to start, but data centres take time, money and effort to set up and run. Google was created in 1998 and its first server was in a dorm room. The first rack of servers was housed by Stanford University. Following that, Google rented co-location services until it commissioned its first data centre in The Dalles, Oregon, built in 2006.

If you don't have a data centre, then setting up in the cloud is an obvious choice. If you do, more questions need to be explored.

2. Does the application have a dynamic workload?

When speaking about dynamic workloads during a given period, like a day or month, does the workload in terms of CPU, memory or storage vary significantly?

An online shop may only become busy during the day and have significantly reduced traffic at night. A vehicle registration service used by a motor dealer may be extremely busy during certain months, and have significantly lower use for others. On the other hand, an accounts package used by the finance department may have an even workload throughout the month, with no major variation.

This becomes more complex when an application is using multiple components or systems (like a reporting system) which ticks along continuously, and it's the component populating the data that peaks and troughs. One system can take advantage of the fluid nature of cloud and the other may well stay in the data centre.

3. Could the application have a dynamic workload?

Many enterprise software companies are now building their platforms with the cloud in mind. For example, Vertica™, a database system. This database system specialises in column-based data and is very quick for big data queries. At its core, it is designed to handle a complete failure of one node and be able to grow or shrink the database nodes in a cluster. This isn't an everyday activity, but it could become one in the near future.

Another example is SAS™, a data analytics platform. The current versions of the platform (9.4) are a little static in nature, but have a feature called the grid, which enables the growth of the computing power of the application as it's required. Again, not very elastic by the hour, but SAS is working on Viya™ which is designed to be cloud native. An upgrade project from a data centre to cloud-based Viya might be cost effective for your organisation.

4. Does your company require more flexibility with storage?

With its appearance of unlimited resources, a cloud provider can provide unlimited storage for your company to store documents, data and other digital assets. Backups can also be stored in the cloud, removing the need for tape and associated issues.

Websites

A great place to start with a proof of concept is the company or internal website (intranet). Development versions of these can be designed and built in the cloud with DevOps best practices in mind. You can start from nothing but a list of requirements, or choose to migrate what you have now and deploy a test environment to the cloud to gain familiarity with the processes and platform.

Enterprise software

Often the hardest to migrate to the cloud is enterprise software. These sometimes monolithic applications expect a very closed and stable environment and may well reside on delicate servers.

While this makes them great candidates for disaster recovery (DR) testing, they are usually the most difficult. I have seen some organisations where a hybrid data centre/public cloud infrastructure exists purely because the enterprise software is unable to be moved or migrated until it's time for a major upgrade.

Many enterprise software vendors are now taking a cloud approach for their newer versions of software, allowing deployments to take advantage of cloud flexibility and cost savings. SAS offers the latest version with DR and scalability designed into the product, providing support for the migration and upgrade project.

Data warehouse and analytics

In 2016 I was helping the MoneySuperMarket Group with their data warehouse and analytics platform. They decided to host it 100% in the cloud as this gave them two major benefits:

1. The cost of running the platform was 30% of what it would cost in the data centre, primarily since the development environments are only available for between eight and twelve hours a day
2. The ability to provision an ever-increasing amount of storage capacity

Using the concepts in this book, the HP Vertica cluster was/is rebuilt every day except for weekends from nothing but the backup of the disks holding the database data, along with the supporting scheduling, ETL (Extract, Transform, Load) and infrastructure servers.

For the AI (Artificial Intelligence) runs, small clusters of servers are provisioned and destroyed on demand to run jobs when required, providing flexibility and saving capital costs on traditional solutions.

Data analysis and Artificial Intelligence

The fastest growing sector is Business Intelligence: using all that data you have stored about your customers to understand what their pain is, what their preferences are, and what are they likely to buy or want to buy next.

Artificial Intelligence is the study of how computers can analyse large amounts of data, and find answers to these and many other questions.

The high availability and scalability of the cloud, along with its ability to store large amounts of data, make it the perfect platform to run the AI algorithms over all your data as quickly as possible.

Platforms such as HP Vertica, Hadoop, R, and programming language frameworks like TensorFlow, enable businesses to create reports, sometimes in real-time, to enable different views of their customers.

Amazon uses its own AI platform to recommend books and other purchases from its massive warehouses based on your and your friends' views and clicks. One of my clients uses click and impression data to drive CRM campaigns which in turn drive sales.

The scalability of the cloud is useful as it can grow as your data grows, or more precisely as the processing time of the data grows. Adding more analytic servers into the cluster reduces the actual clock time by spreading the processing over more workers, much like scaling the back end of an application.

Application design for cloud operations

Services are applications that run from network or internet facing servers, and are usually long running. For example, a web or email server. Services are another component of an overall enterprise level application. For instance, a three-layer application will have at least three services. The database service, the application or business logic web service, and the customer facing or website service.

Separating out the monolithic application in this way gives us more flexibility in deployment to provide better resiliency against failure, and the ability to upgrade the application component or the server infrastructure it runs on.

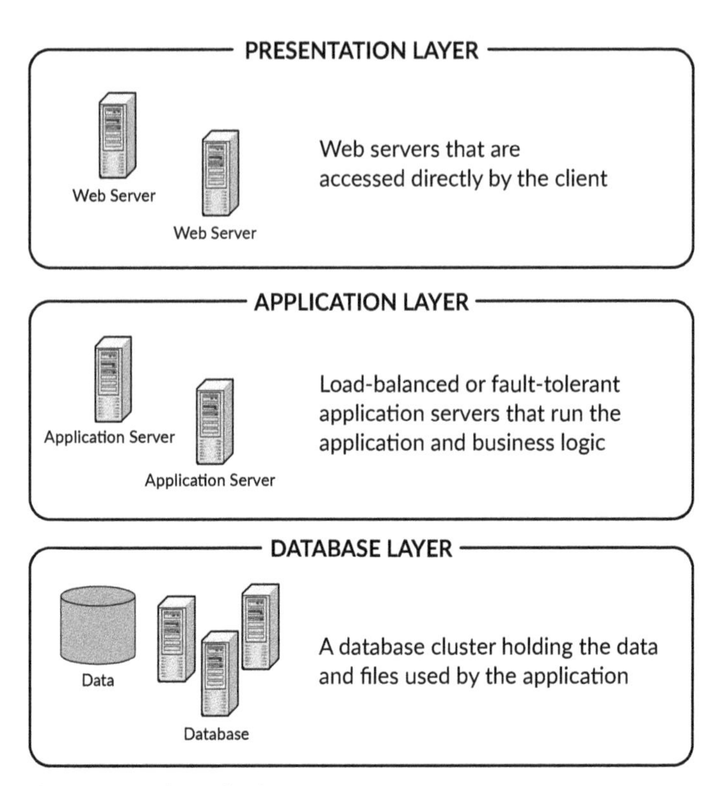

Figure 3.2: *A 3-tier application*

When designing an application for the cloud, the functional parts of the application are usually broken down into the smallest component possible and referred to as micro architecture. This is the exact opposite of monolithic, where the whole of the application needs to reside on the biggest server hardware you can imagine, with hard coded dependencies everywhere.

In addition to creating small discrete components of the application, some care also needs to be considered in order for the components to communicate. Shared data sources or message queues can facilitate this and need to be considered and figured into the design. Breaking the application into smaller pieces not only aids in the scaling of the application, it also helps with development and testing.

With each of the components comes a design or story, defined inputs and outputs, a list of resources the component can expect to use, and a testing plan for ensuring quality of the produced module.

Developing in this way can make use of personal Docker™ – a tool that provides isolation between applications – or other virtual environments to develop and test, further increasing velocity by reducing contention on shared resources.

In a micro architecture design, all parts of the application are designed to run on their own, providing inputs and outputs just for that function. This allows two main things to happen. The first is that each component can be developed independently of any other part, including testing. The second is that it can also be deployed independently – and often in a scalable manner – allowing the application to avoid performance bottlenecks as each independent component can be designed with scaling built in.

If you are used to running applications in data centres, you know a lot of thought and design goes into getting the right server or servers to run the application. This is usually based on factors like growth, storage and estimated future demand of that service. Within the design for the application or service, it's assumed the functionality won't change very much.

IT consultancies and project managers first introduced change control to reduce the change of the application in order to keep things as static as the quotes and project plan had predicted.

When moving to the cloud, one of the major benefits (and potential headaches) comes from the expected rate of change an application can have. The Unicorn businesses have pivoted mid-project to move along a different path to create an even better and more profitable plan.

This flexibility is a million miles away from traditional data centres and project management, so it will take some time to get used to. However, once the idea of rapid development has taken hold, the cloud can be easily embraced to empower your teams and your application.

Dependencies

From the very simplest programs to apps that run on your mobile phone, to the largest enterprise applications running on servers, mainframes and office computers, code is made up of the same structure – of which the function is one of the smallest components.

The very smallest component is a machine code instruction. These run on the CPU itself and are made up of three types: math, decisions (or comparators) and moving data. It's rare for programmers to deal at the CPU level, and they usually focus on statements. These statements vary between programming languages, and are functions turned into machine language by a compiler or interpreter.

A programming language will give the developer a range of instruction functions that mirror the CPU instructions. Mathematical calculations, program flow (comparators) and moving data (input or output) can be wrapped in our own function definitions, thereby simplifying the code by building on top of other code. This makes it easier to build more complicated programs by reusing code that we have already written or is available.

```
1 | #include <iostream>
2 | using namespace std;
3 |
4 | int main () {
5 | // for loop execution
6 | for( int a = 10; a < 20; a = a + 1 ) {
7 |   cout << "value of a: " << a << endl;
8 | }
9 |
10 | return 0;
11 | }
```

In this simple snippet, we can see the basics:

1. A function, `main()` on line 4, which contains, on line 6, a 'for' loop (program flow)

2. On line 6, variables (for holding data) and calculations (`a = a + 1`)

3. Finally, on line 7, moving data by outputting it to the screen (cout function)

A function takes the input, manipulates or stores the data, and produces an output. Some functions need no input and just produce output, like an initialiser function that will output a data structure that the application will use later.

A function may take an input and create an output, like a mathematical function, or it could take an input but not create an output: a no operation or wait function might do this.

Programming languages usually come with standard libraries, which build on basic functions, saving time and effort for the developer. In the example above, the iostream library is included to give the program access to the cout function.

As a developer, custom libraries of functions can be written and shared. As new functions are added to these libraries, they are version-controlled so that developers using the library can expect certain functions to exist and work in specific ways, based on the version number that has been downloaded and installed.

Writing a program using functions from a library can reduce development time. However, as libraries are updated with new functions, features and bug fixes, the specific version number is very important to the program working reliably.

Dependencies on libraries and other assets (like fonts or graphics) are managed by the developer. Tracking these can be difficult when one library depends on another library. Without careful management, dependency hell can ensue while trying to keep these interdependencies up to date.

It's these interdependencies that can make it difficult to deploy an application and software to a computer or server. Many programming languages have a package manager to look after these interdependencies for the developer. Ruby uses bundler, Python uses PIP. By creating a Ruby GEMFILE in the application project, running the bundle command to read this file will install the specified versions of libraries, as well as ensuring the interdependent libraries are also installed. If there's a conflict, this needs to be resolved by the developer.

You've probably seen shared library installation in action yourself when you run an application installer on your computer or laptop. The installer, as well as installing the application itself, will also install dependency programs and libraries. On some occasions, this can cause previously installed software to break as it was using the same but different version of the shared library.

Installing applications to servers is no different, and where two different programs require different versions of the same shared library, a second server needs to be deployed to keep the programs separate.

Application isolation

When having a second server or computer isn't practical we can employ application isolation. This is where some of the computer is partitioned off, at least at the file system level, which will allow two programs with conflicting dependencies to exist on the same machine. On the Citrix servers I configured for Sanctuary Housing, the challenge was to migrate Microsoft Office to the latest version. The solution chosen in this case was to use an application isolation application called Softgrid.

This application, acquired by Microsoft in 2006, is called Microsoft Application Virtualisation. The App-V stack sandboxes the execution environment so that an application doesn't make changes directly to the underlying operation system and file system, but rather is contained in a bubble.

A technology known as containers performs a similar function to enable applications and services to run in a bubble – also known as a container. Docker provides isolation between applications. It does simplify the deployment to a degree: however, with the cheap and abundant availability of virtual machines, especially those built with the immutable model, deploying to containers is as easy as building a new cloud server.

There's a growing desire for the server aspect to be completely obfuscated from the developers, thus allowing the developer to deliver a working container and easing deployment. Amazon Web Services provides a serverless product that runs on top of their container management service to enable the easy deployment of these images and containers. With the ease at which virtual servers can be built and destroyed, Application design with the twelve factor Application principles, and cloud architecture, servers or containers can provide a stable and well-performing platform for your network service.

Automated and self-serve development environments

Imagine a server is built from code and in an automated way, duplication of a server is easy, and while the initial development may take longer, you have faith that it can be replaced easily and quickly when the time comes. This is true for development and production level servers and services. Having the definitions of your servers in code (Infrastructure as Code, IaC) enables the automatic provisioning of server roles.

Often configuration is split into roles, such as web server, database server or application server. With these roles defined, your development team can request one or many servers based on these templates, and the request will take only minutes. This removes obstacles and friction, giving your developers a production-like environment for them to write, test and deploy their code. This in turn allows the teams to deliver quicker and faster, with production-ready and fully tested code, for your customers.

Having a reliable development environment that you can destroy and rebuild, enables the trust needed to save money on the weekends.

Saving money

The cloud enables a pay-for-what-you-use model. This enables services to run idle on a small footprint if the service isn't experiencing a high load. This in turn saves money by not running unnecessary compute resources.

When you know you can have a working server set up in minutes or seconds, it doesn't seem too hard to switch it off and destroy it when you or your team have gone home for the night or weekend. Running the servers during the week saves you over 25% of the cost of running a server in the cloud because you're not running on – and therefore not paying for – the weekends.

MoneySuperMarket ended up with a similar solution after my team set up a system for creating and destroying the Data Lake development environments every day. The server roles were well defined, the data was backed up, and at 7.00 pm every night the servers would shut down and be destroyed. For the next eleven hours, they were not charged for servers. Then at 6.00 am the automation would kick in and build the whole dev environment, restore the data, ready for the teams at 8.00 am. To the team it was if they had never been switched off. To the finance department, they just saved nearly 50% of the server spend for that team. When you consider the automated build didn't do anything on Saturday or Sunday, the cost falls to thirteen hours × five days vs. twenty-four hours × seven days, resulting in only 38% of full-time running costs.

Application high availability and performance

Scaling in, down, up and out

Handling more demand from your customers can be tackled in one of two ways: bigger servers or more servers. This section will share the pros and cons of each.

Autoscaling clusters not only ensures your application is serving your customers, but it can do it without staff intervention. With some situations, planning may be required to make it smoother – for instance if you're about to run an advertising campaign.

CASE STUDY: AXA WEB APP SCALING AND LOAD BALANCING CASE STUDY

One of the web server applications run by AXA company runs on a typical.NET stack; there's a load balancer in front of the user facing web servers, balancing load between the two front-end servers. A few users of the system would state that they sometimes had to log in more than once while using the system. This occurred when the load balancer deemed one of the servers too busy and would switch the user's session to the other server.

It would only do this at peak periods due to sticky sessions: the load balancer would fill up one server first, then start sending sessions to the other servers.

The web servers had been set up to store the user's session data in a shared database cluster instance. As per best practice, this data was encrypted in the database. Due to an oversight in the initial configuration of the servers, each server had its own encryption key and thus could not decrypt any sessions created by the other server. Once identified, the fix was easy. The development team worked quickly through the test environments to implement a shared key in the application.

It was also found that once the servers shared the session data using the same key, the sessions were no longer required to be sticky and the load was more evenly balanced across the two servers.

Data persistence

A cloud-first application is said to follow the design principles laid out in the twelve factor application.[3]

This is a methodology which includes:

- **Processes:** Execute the app as one or more stateless processes
- **Concurrency:** Scale out via the process model
- **Disposability:** Maximise robustness with fast start-up and graceful shutdown
- **Dev/prod parity:** Keep development, staging and production as similar as possible
- **Logs:** Treat logs as event streams

3 https://12factor.net

Most of these reinforce the notion of short-lived, disposable and stateless servers.

This presents a few challenges with storage of data. In flexible and on-demand environments, some of the data is needed so tasks can pick up from where they left off; databases, file stores and content for example. In the design of the environment will be the need to persist data from one server to the next in the event the entire environment is switched off overnight between rebuilds.

Keeping this data accessible and fresh requires some thought, as in our 'everything could fail' scenario. That data will need to be in at least two places to sustain a failure of the disks. Once it's in at least two places, keeping the two places coordinated presents another situation to overcome.

FIVE

Problems

In the previous chapter we covered some great features of cloud deployments, but unless the application and staff resource are running with DevOps and Agile values, the business could invest without seeing a great return.

With the cloud model you only pay for what you use, and matching demand saves money compared to the persistent model where you would have to provision servers at maximum capacity all the time.

However, due to this transient nature, in addition to hardware failures and aggressive money saving deals where you can bid for spare capacity for a much cheaper price, your server needs to be able to recover quickly from failures. This must be considered when designing the infrastructure and application for deployment to the cloud.

Built to fail is a paradigm you must adopt. Google and Amazon build their own servers as cheaply as possible knowing that even if they used name brand servers, components fail at least 4% during the first year – and this increases as the server and components get older.[4] If you're going to get a failure anyway, why not save money and design around the failure.

Disaster recovery

A cluster gives your application a certain level of resilience against failure, and gives your team time to replace or perform routine maintenance on any one of the nodes in a cluster.

While it's possible to have a cluster of one server, in most cases this doesn't give any protection against failure of that server. Clusters of two or three servers

4 www.statista.com/statistics/430769/annual-failure-rates-of-servers/

usually have a much larger number of nodes possible, depending on the software running on them.

It's best practice that all cluster nodes are as close to identical as possible. Of course, some differences will exist, such as internal hostname and IP addresses; however, the software installed (and the versions) should be exactly the same. Configuration control gives you that certainty here also.

To help this, Amazon Web Services and VMWare provide the ability to create a template server image from which to build your new nodes, and keep differences to a minimum; this also brings the mean time to recovery or build time for the node to a very short time. As you will see later, this can be important.

When the server fails it can be rebuilt in under thirty minutes. The state and software configuration can be well tested across several environments, and with certain settings and application versions, to ensure compatibility. They can be built on demand, enabling either a scheduled provision of service, ie 8am to 6pm, or based on current workload, for instance, more customers means more servers.

IT failures happen, and being prepared makes the path to recovery quick and painless. Working in the cloud makes this more important as its flexible nature gives rise to temporary working, and physical failure is still a risk.

This is in addition to any backup scheme you have in place, and should be tested regularly as an insurance policy: when you need it, you'll be glad you planned ahead.

Monitoring of the servers and system components for both performance and failures will give an early indication that something needs attention or repair. Having alerts on the monitoring system usually raises an incident with whoever happens to be on-call. The worst aspect of working in operations is the on-call rotation: once an error is detected, a human is called – usually in the middle of the night – to fix the problem.

This manual process, like most processes, can be automated. The automated build process removes some of the stress; however, when building an environment many fail-safe and redundant features can be employed to make any failure a line in a report, rather than a business impacting event.

SPOFs

Single Points of Failure (SPOFs) are components in your application that, if they fail, will cause catastrophic or total failure of your application to deliver its output and results to your customers and users.

Examples of SPOFs:

- They can be designed into the application, such as a single write-only database server, or created by accident, eg a new feature requiring access to a legacy database which is seldom accessed, and where the application checks for access on every run and complains if it isn't there.
- The database server isn't clustered as it's only running on one server, which means if that server fails, the on-call engineer will have fun using backups to build and restore a replacement.

Limitations of budget and/or hardware is often a cause of these issues, so in the flexible cloud environment you can remove these dependencies.

Having SPOFs isn't the end of your application. It may be acceptable that if the component can be recovered quickly enough in the event of a failure, the impact will be reduced or minimal.

AWS removes most SPOFs and gives you the option of duplicating parts of your application infrastructure to redundant sections of the cloud – where you can be sure that any faults are isolated due to the placement of your servers.

For instance, in the AWS London Region (eu-west-2) there are at least two Availability Zones that are independent from each other with separate data, power and storage – and these have a fast network link between them to allow clusters to communicate effectively. With a server in each zone, any component, including the zone, could fail with a greatly reduced impact.

Data

Replacing a server is easy. Replacing data, not so much. In the cloud and cluster environment it's not enough to have multiple servers – you must ensure data is replicated or sharded (in a database) in a way that any failure is seamless, and recovery is automatic.

For static data, this is a simple case of having at least two stores of the information and copying this to the servers on creation. Depending on the size of the data, this could significantly increase boot to serve time.

For dynamic data, such as that in a database, replication in a cluster can save the system from some failures. Vertica (Column Storage database) uses a type of RAID (Redundant Array of Inexpensive Disks) to not only speed up queries, but also to guard against a node or multiple nodes failing.

Database sharding is also a popular practice, where related data is stored together and replicated between two or more services. Elastic Search is a good example of this kind of data redundancy.

Configuration creep

Long uptimes used to be the holy grail of stability. If your server didn't need a reboot for days or months, this was perceived as a badge of honour. But the longer a server exists, the more changes occur on that server, leading to a creep of the configuration from when it was built. In the case of clusters, where manual maintenance occurs, this can lead to cluster nodes no longer being identical. This can cause corruptions, spurious errors and make additions to expand the cluster, or replacement in the event of failures, difficult or even impossible.

During my time at Sanctuary Housing, a project called for the use of a new database. As the database needed some redundancy, rather than building a new database cluster, the existing Microsoft SQL server cluster was to be expanded and needed an extra node to handle the extra workload.

As this was a physical on premises cluster new hardware was ordered. Since it had been a few years since the original nodes had been built, this was a newer model. It shouldn't have presented much of a problem, as this was from a major hardware vendor, the specification of the server was nearly the same, save for some updated component, like CPU, motherboard revision and BIOS updates.

While waiting for the new server to arrive, paperwork and processes were followed to create a change window. For the duration of the upgrade, the cluster would have some downtime and affect the existing applications that relied on that server. Due to the ease of creating new servers, each application would have its own cluster now.

The server was deployed with the operating system by the first stage automation. The rest of the new server configuration was done by following the documentation for the cluster and verified with the master node. At this point the new server was nearly ready to meet its new colleagues.

The plan was set, and this wasn't the first time a new node had been added to a windows cluster. As it involved software installation, server reboots, networking setup and configuration, we opted for an overnight change window that started after business hours. As the change window approached, we ate pizza in preparation for the task ahead.

However, one of the nodes didn't match the configuration close enough for the cluster to form a quorum. The software complained about a mismatch. We tried everything during the generous change window. As it approached midnight, we were getting tired and the server was still not welcome as a new node in the cluster. In the end, we had to back out the changes and restore the cluster in its prior state, abandoning the new node expansion.

Delicate servers and services

In some situations, where a server is difficult to build and configure, some actions are difficult to replicate even with the best documentation. This can lead to a delicate server, where perhaps the knowledge to keep it running lays in only one or two staff and can easily take days to recover when failure occurs.

Decommissioning of this server may be part of a bigger project. What about migration?

Moving the server to a virtual infrastructure reduces the risk associated with hardware failure. This doesn't have to mean the cloud. Should your organisation have a VMWare cluster available, this would be a sensible first step. With the threat of hardware failure appeased, some of the risk is removed.

Migration of the server to the cloud gives other options, such as a full server snapshot every day, with the hope that should the worst happen, at least the server can be restored to the day before.

The long-term solution would be to migrate the roles away from the server over time. Unless this is a monolithic application, decommissioning or replacement should be considered.

Service discovery and DNS

A core infrastructure component allows your customers and components of the application to find endpoints. These are points or addresses that provide the interface into the application.

DNS, Domain Name System, was created in 1983 as a way of resolving names like mail.example.com or www.google.com to IP addresses, so that the network connection could be established. Before this, networks were small enough to enable Stanford Research Institute to maintain a text file to do the mapping called hosts.txt. This approach is still used in small private networks.

There are millions of domains, containing millions of websites. DNS enables us to go to a website without worrying about where it is. To make this process quick, a lot of DNS data is cached and managed by what DNS calls TTL (Time To Live). For static servers this works fine; however, if internally your tier three or four, or microservice application lives on short-lived cloud servers or containers within Docker or Kubernetes™, this caching could cause the application to fail due to stale information.

The answer to this is service discovery. Essentially this set of tools enables the component to register its address with a central service and a monitoring service, and if it's busy, overloads or dies, a deregistration process kicks in, enabling only good services to be found, with the bad service records removed from the system.

Consul™ provides all the above for your services. It provides additional functions too; however, I would be clear on what you want each installation to do and keep things simple with one installation per role or task.

Another approach is a somewhat custom tool, where the server registers itself with a dynamic DNS service, such as AWS Route 53, with a short monitoring cycle, that renews the subscription say every five minutes. Using Sensu and plugins will be able to do this.

Costs

A word of warning: just migrating existing servers and running them twenty-four hours a day, seven days a week may end up costing you more than a comparable data centre based server.

Cloud providers will provide discounts if a service usage is committed to. AWS enables reserved instances. These are credits that you pay for upfront and get a discount on the hourly rate. GCP gives a discount based on the instance's uptime: the longer it's up, the bigger the discount.

For example, maybe you agree to pay for a specific size of AWS instance for three years, based on 100% usage or uptime. Committing to this timeframe earns you a discount on the regular on-demand price, which can be further reduced if you're willing to pay for a certain chunk of the bill upfront.

Amazon Web Services also provides the facility to request a spot instance. Due to the number of physical machines in each data centre, if there's spare capacity this is auctioned off using the Vickrey auction method. This means a server is provided at a low price, but if the demand rises, the server will be shut down if your maximum bid is not high enough. This is useful if the server can work on jobs that can be interrupted.

As the cloud is a pay-as-you-go service, savings are easily achievable if you exploit its elastic nature.

In addition to using spot instances, having a scheduled time for the servers to be available can provide significant savings over constant use.

SECTION 3

SOLVING CLOUD PROBLEMS

SIX

System Development

The full Systems Development Life Cycle (SDLC) follows the inception to grave lifetime of a product. The basic steps for the full software cycle are inception, planning, analysis, design, implementation, maintenance and decommission (grave).

Unless you are working at a start-up, some of the infrastructure required for software development will exist already. I will cover this shortly in DevOps environments.

A project (or indeed a start-up) will have some sort of spark idea or workshop that starts with its inception. Planning requires an approach based on products rather than projects. This perspective focuses on the entire lifetime of any product created, which is quite different to a project lifecycle to create something new or as a replacement. I see lots of legacy applications within organisations because decommissioning is not part of the project that replaces the superseded application.

For agile application development the steps are:

Inception

Inception includes determining the initial and clear idea of what the system or software is to provide.

- What problem will this solve?
- Who is the audience, customers, stakeholders, etc?
- What features should the minimum viable product have?
- What funding is available for the lifetime of the system?

In many ways these are like the questions posed by a new business start-up. I've seen larger businesses create a separate entity to facilitate delivery of a new thing without the overhead of the larger organisation.

DevOps environments

Alongside the discovery and design steps of a project, the developer, infrastructure and server environments are also designed and set up. This foundation layer contains a few key services required in any setup and a few that may be bespoke for the application.

Developer environment

The bare minimum for the developers to produce effectively is a CI system such as Jenkins and a source code repository such as Gitlab. These can be provisioned privately, or public services can be used. This will also be required to store configuration information and to enable the automation of infrastructure testing and build.

Infrastructure environment

This contains basic services. This list can be longer or shorter depending on the product delivery, and as a starter, it looks like this:

- **Network design and security:** At the design level, the application or service will exist in a network and some of it isn't required to be public. Part of the network design shows where components exist at a network level, and these network subnets need to be created in line with the design and for expansion.

- **DNS and service discovery:** AWS provides public DNS to its subnets, but if you're interfacing with an internal organisation, you may need further services. AWS Route53 does offer internal DNS, so this may be utilised. Service discovery comes in the form of Route53 scripts. Other solutions, including Consul, may be helpful for tighter service discovery with monitoring and support for flexible environments.

- **Secrets and Certificate Authority:** All traffic between microservices should be encrypted with TLS, and while self-signed certificates are okay for the proof of concept stage, when clients are connecting to the service a trusted certificate will be required. Tied closely with this is secret storage for a secure way for application and service components to collect secrets and sensitive information required by the service.

- **Artefact and repository caches:** During the application build processes, binaries and artefacts are created prior to deployment. These can be stored in a version-controlled environment ready for the deploy process to pull them. In addition, should internet access not be readily available, caches for various repositories are also advisable. While many mirrors exist for Centos, Ruby Gems and Pypi, you may wish to have a local copy to improve stability and to build servers or images from.
- **Automated image creation:** To speed up the build and recovery of servers, an automated process to create server images, while not needed early in the project, will speed up production deployments. I would recommend Packer from Hashicorp.
- **Monitoring and logging:** During the software development cycle and production operations, the application will be logging information and performance metrics so that bugs can be captured and bottlenecks can be rectified. This information is best collated in a central logging area, so that displays can be given and retained for analysis after the server has been replaced. This system will also alert support when something has been

discovered as malfunctioning or server limits are being tested. Examples that can be utilised are Elasticsearch with Logstash and Kibana (for storing the data), Sensu (for metrics and alerting), and Smashing (for dashboards).

Discovery, research and development

Most projects start at this stage with the foundations already set up. During this time, user requirements are gathered, tested and researched, and a clear idea of the problem to be solved and the minimum viable product is sketched out.

Following an iterative development process, the servers and software are set up to deliver value to the client one step at a time. This can be off the shelf or enterprise software as well as complete custom-made applications.

During this phase, testing and continuous integration are important as ever in order to get feedback from the systems and the customers to ensure value is being added. When the solution is mature enough, which might be days or weeks depending on the complexity of the initial steps, it's deployed to production.

Production

A system doesn't stop development just because it's in production. However, the non-functional requirements are usually more important when the service is in production or public facing. This is where the monitoring of performance, and the logging of metrics and errors, provides vital feedback to the development teams while providing the best possible service to the customer.

Maintenance

Further to the development release cycle continuing to upgrade the production system at whatever rate your organisation is comfortable with, the performance and security of the system also requires maintenance.

The dependencies on your servers will be experiencing upgrades as new bugs are fixed and security patches released. In addition, should the customer base for the application grow, then performance metrics will be assessed to ensure that enough servers are available to keep response times within acceptable levels.

Decommission

Finally, when the application comes to the end of its life due to major upgrades or replacement, the legacy is decommissioned. Often this step is missed as it's usually far removed from the team setting up the system. However, it's an important step to save the company money from the costs associated with maintenance and an application that is no longer providing value.

My Four Steps for a successful cloud deployment

Step one: Application designed for cloud

As the cloud is a pay-as-you-go service, the application should be too. AWS's CTO Werner Vogels speaking at Amazon re:Invent said 'While an Amazon EC2 instance might look like a server to you, it is not a server. It is something you can switch off, it is a software component.'

With a disposable approach to servers and therefore the services that run on them, this means considering start time, ungraceful shutdown, where the data lives, and automation.

Many applications designed to run on cloud can recover from infrastructure failure by building themselves quickly, avoiding stateful and important data stored on the servers wherever possible, replicating data to preserve it, and doing all this with as little human interaction as possible.

For the infrastructure do this, DevOps borrowed from developers and created automated programs to do the heavy lifting involved in building server environments and recovering.

By moving to a programmable model and storing the instructions to build the infrastructure in the form of executable instructions, the servers can build and recover themselves. This is known as Infrastructure as Code.

Imagine the instructions ready to be executed for an installation of SAS, where at the click of a button and a few parameters, an environment or service group of servers is created, built, configured and commissioned ready to work. This repeatable program empowers the developers to create their own version of the production servers, so that whatever they create and test is working in a way that the production version of that service is configured.

This is because both have been created from the same code and instructions. This immediately removes the complexity and risk associated with deploying to production, as it has been tested and running in a near duplicate.

This infrastructure code is designed with cloud failures in mind to enable fast recovery. As it is code, it can be tested.

A tool for defining and running code to create infrastructure is called Terraform by Hashicorp. This is an open source tool owned by the community. With a collaboration mindset, this project is alive with updates. This tool enables instructions to be written, accessing providers of cloud services, AWS, GCP, Azure, with new features added to the tool as quickly as it can be ordered via the cloud provider's API.

Once the infrastructure and servers have been created, the servers need to be configured. The three leading tools for this are Puppet, Chef and Ansible. All three can be used in an immutable way, allowing the servers to build themselves and enabling fast scaling and recovery from failure.

Step two: Automated infrastructure for your build, test, deployment and operation

With the infrastructure definitions available as code, the process to deploy the infrastructure can use the same methodology as the developers, to build, test and deploy using pipelines. This does mean the tests have to be written with the infrastructure code, but once this is done it gives a massive safety net for the team: great tests mean more reliable code and more reliable operations.

In this way the infrastructure code can be tested in the same way as the application code. Developers in the same team as DevOps enables this close circuit of testing and feedback, providing faster and shorter deployments through automation.

For this to work best DevOps needs an infrastructure development environment. This enables build and testing of infrastructure code without getting in the way of the developers.

Nothing tests code like deployments, so once the infrastructure tests have been completed successfully a deployment as often as you can should occur. In one team I worked with, the four development environments (including the DevOps environment) included the same code (with different versions) which rippled through each morning.

Every day the environments would be built by a continuous deployment pipeline in Jenkins with the infrastructure and developer code. This enabled massive confidence in the code by the time it reached pre-production and live.

Alongside any new features and services was a test to ensure it worked as planned, as well as further tests to monitor the application behaviour and status as it was running. An essential part of deployment is operations. It's at this step that monitoring of the servers, services and applications gives peace of mind that all is okay, or in the event of a failure, a quick and precise clue as to what component has failed. Just another fast feedback loop for improvement.

Having a dashboard with coloured boxes and graphs to show status and performance is a great thing for the work area – and for everyone to see and keep an eye on. Anything red on the dashboard will get attention by the team long before any symptoms show in the application itself. This is partly due to the fault tolerance built into the servers and the application, and partly for the users to notice.

As an aid to diagnosing performance issues, save application log information to a file or output stream. This valuable information needs to be stored safely, and since we're operating in a disposable environment, somewhere other than the server the application is running on. The popular ELK or Elastic stack will certainly help. Not only does it store logs efficiently, more importantly, it allows for the easy searching and interrogation of those logs.

No deployment would be complete without a way for users to find the service they need. In a microservice application, there can be many such moving parts. Service discovery is the technology used to track where these parts are so the application or users can find the relevant pieces. DNS can perform this task, but as mentioned earlier, Consul may well be best for your systems.

It's worth mentioning Docker at this point. Using this tool simplifies the development and deployment of software components by wrapping them up in a self-sufficient unit, which enables the deployment to be as easy for production as it is for any other environment on its path through testing. Be wary of local data in the Docker container though, and as for any cloud application, local data is discouraged.

Step three: Scaling for flexible workloads

One of the most attractive features of moving to the cloud is the ability to scale applications quickly based on workload. This burst feature enables the systems to call on extra resources when needed, and possibly more importantly, release them once the demand drops so you're not paying for servers to sit idle.

There are three parts to enabling this function for your application:

- Access points or load balancers
- Monitoring and automation systems
- Tuned metrics to control or trigger the automatic scaling up and down

Access points or load balancers provide a clear point of entry to the application. For a web server, this is what sits behind the website address, but in front of the web servers producing the web pages. Having a known entry point means the application can divert the request to wherever is best to deal with that action at that time.

As mentioned in the AXA web app scaling and load balancing case study, the application may need some awareness of the load balancer – so they work together. This may require some design and development time to ensure the APIs and microservices can reconnect (in the event a server disappears mid-query) or share data appropriately knowing the server is in a team.

The monitoring and automation systems are then made ready to enable multiple services to be created and destroyed based on demand automatically. Auto scaling is where the automation follows rules based on some metric describing the performance of the application, so that resources are added and taken away for consistent response times.

Scaling out and in relies on a rule. This rule is based on a metric, CPU usage, user requests or memory usage. This metric must be chosen carefully for its ability to measure the load on the servers if it's to increase service capacity when required.

Scaling out is easy – scaling in, however, is a little trickier. Servers and applications create data, either just logs and activity or new inputs such as photos or status updates. I will talk about data in a moment. The other thing that makes scaling in difficult is when to judge that the server is no longer needed or being accessed by your customers. A simple delay in the rule's execution will help slow the automation so it doesn't react to a sudden spike or drop in traffic, where the demand would have changed before the server can start or stop.

The load balancer will be able to stop traffic going to a server when it's no longer needed – this is called draining connections. Once this is complete, the server can shut down. The application may also need modification to allow this, ensuring that a user connection doesn't need to stay connected to any server specifically due to local data.

Step four: Keeping the data safe

Twelve factor applications introduced in chapter four discourage any form of local data. Keeping data local to a server may be easier and quicker, but it restricts the options for scaling and providing redundancy for the information.

Some applications, by default, expect local data on the server. In the cloud, we cannot afford this luxury for two reasons: should we allow local data, it will be lost when the server scales in, or if a fault occurs causing the server to be withdrawn from service.

Local data as opposed to shared data is required in some circumstances and must be designed to be disposable. Most services require a database. While this is not stored on the application server and is shared, the server hosting the database service itself needs some form of local data to store that data. Most database systems can be deployed in such a way that it acts as part of a cluster and can survive any one node in that cluster disappearing through scaling or fault. Automated systems should then rebuild a replacement node, degrading the service while this takes place for efficient completion.

Other forms of local data must be configured away from their defaults to enable remote storage.

Application activity and error logs should be streamed to a central logging service. This should be extended to all logging on the server, including system logs and application logs. Not only does this keep the data safe (assuming the logging service is itself a cluster), it also enables easy searching and aggregation of the data for analysis and reporting.

Sometimes overlooked are temporary files used by the server and application. This may be related to a user's session, but it restricts the user to that one server, making it difficult to scale in.

In some cases, such as WordPress websites, the data directories can only be synchronised if the application can be modified by in-house developers to use shared storage. NFS, Resilio or another syncing solution should be used to preserve and share the data among the application servers.

Keeping data off the application servers and limited to the shared data servers allows for better disaster recovery, enabling a focused effort on the data services for backup and quick service restoration following a component failure.

Having the data in a cluster will protect the service from hardware failure, but a bigger disaster may require relocation of the service entirely. Data backups will enable recovery of data to a different site should the very worst happen. For this reason, cloud providers have multiple sites or regions, and data can be copied or backed up to another physical location. Having the infrastructure code ready to execute this alternative region is a worthy exercise should the cost of total loss of service justify it.

Regular backup of the data is important for micro restores. This is where only part of the data, otherwise known as a granular restore, will provide a point in time restoration following corruption or malicious data loss. The shorter backup interval reduces the actual data loss endured in these situations, but will take some thought to set up.

Using the cloud as an offsite backup solution for an existing data centre is more reliable and cheaper than traditional tape and shipping solutions. Tapes are not reliable when it comes to restores, and the process by which the tapes are recovered before restoring can be lengthy, making the cloud an attractive option.

CASE STUDY: DOCKER HOST ENCRYPTION

Almost all applications require secrets or configuration data to function. Username and passwords to databases, encryption keys, and company specific information. One of my clients stored this information in a private source code repository but wanted it to be encrypted, obviously. The server operations team had access to the encryption keys but, being a busy team, wanted a way for the developers to be in charge of their own secrets and source code.

Definition of done: have a self-service portal that developers can use to generate encrypted strings of sensitive configuration data to be included in source code. The portal should include an API, so the deployment pipeline can request this information to be committed by the developer.

There were a few other constraints, for example that it must be written in a language that can be supported by the rest of the team. Ruby was chosen, and the deployment was to be a Docker container. A Linux virtual machine was provided with Docker, Git and Ruby pre-installed. This was an immutable server in AWS built using Masterless Puppet from an infrastructure repository in GitHub. A mixture of Rubymine to Git and using Docker integration allowed for the development of a Sinatra (Ruby web application framework) app to be developed.

The solution involved three Docker containers working together providing SSL/TLS certificates for the web server app and API, a data volume that held the public encryption keys, and the application container that ran the web services. Joining the three containers in this way enabled each to be updated independently of the others. If the PKI changed, slot in another container. Need to rotate the encryption keys? Update the keys and rebuild the container image.

For testing, another stub or dummy container was added for the mail transport. As no authentication was available for the application to use, a secure way of sending the encrypted string was email addresses restricted to a domain suffix.

The application also exposed the logs, requests and usage information to Docker so that another container would grab them and funnel them off to a central statistics and logging service.

How does this example follow the four steps?

By developing and deploying in Docker, cloud deployment was enabled. Having the application stateless, by not having a login, meant a form was submitted to the API and sent an email, so it was scalable.

The code repository contained a Dockerfile, which a Jenkins job would build, push the image to a private Docker registry, invoke the infrastructure code to ensure a DockerHost was available, then deploy the Docker images to it. This pipeline could be triggered when an update occurred. This automation provided a one-click deployment for the developer.

The self-contained nature of the Docker containers and images meant that it could be scaled and duplicated as required. The data inputs were not cached anywhere, and the output was immediately dispatched by email. The only data to worry about was the logs exposed to the central logging service.

SEVEN

Automation

My highest value is fun, and 'Automate manual and monotonous tasks' has become my mantra, so we can focus on and have more fun.

In this and the following chapters, I will share the method and technologies that I use every day to automate data centre and cloud services, as well as Amazon's cloud services.

> 'You cannot automate a process that does not exist.'
> – IBM

Before we can go about automating a process, we must understand how to do it manually. You must be able to do something manually and in small easy steps, so simple that you can tell a computer how to do it. I've read in many business books (like *The E-Myth Revisited: Why Most Small Businesses Don't Work and What to do About it* and *Traction: Get a Grip on Your Business*), that many businesses run more smoothly with an operations manual that allows any staff member to perform the functions.

We can take that manual and automate the process with the use of technology. This in turn makes the company more efficient through reduced errors and costs. Not all tasks can be automated, but I believe that that is just a limitation of the technology available today.

Self-driving cars and drones are already here to help us in the physical world, and software has been around for a bit longer to help us with automatic processes. Both Netflix and Amazon utilise automation and AI processes to recommend that next film or book. Applications, computer games and bots provide useful service outside of businesses too.

As I mentioned earlier, when I was working for a national social housing provider, a rite of passage was to build a Citrix server. The architecture of IT was that of dumb terminals installed in remote sites that were not much more than a screen with a keyboard and mouse. All the computer power was provided by central servers with many of the staff sharing a server with a desktop for them to see on their local screen. These central servers ran Citrix and Terminal Services.

Setting up a new Citrix server involved taking a brand-new server out of the box from HP, installing the CPUs, memory and disks, then fitting this into a server rack in the data centre. After plugging in the various essential cables and switching it on, a small automation process would load Microsoft Windows onto the new server, then the technician would follow a list of instructions to complete the configuration.

Initially this was manageable. However, as the company grew bigger, building one or two servers a week wasn't enough, and more technology was deployed to automate more of the steps.

The physical aspects of server setup are reduced with virtual servers, and cloud providers make it no longer necessary. Thanks to advances in CPU and computer capacity modern servers are very powerful. To improve efficiency and utilisation of hardware (physical computers), virtualisation is a way of running more than two logical computers in an isolated way (they are not aware they are sharing) on the same physical computer and therefore share some of the capacity of that machine. This gives cost savings through better utilisation of hardware, space, cooling and other physical requirements, while delivering the same level of results from the virtual servers.

Many businesses already have data centres of their own and run virtual workloads with technology from VMWare, Citrix Xen and Microsoft. Private cloud refers to the ability of internal staff to order virtual servers on demand, without the direct intervention of IT or using an external public cloud.

To facilitate and manage virtual servers, there are public cloud providers where you can purchase virtual servers on a pay-as-you-go basis. They also manage the infrastructure, data centres, network, etc – removing a lot of the admin and miscellaneous overheads.

Amazon Web Services (AWS) is the world's biggest public cloud provider. Created for Amazon.com, AWS is the infrastructure that Amazon uses itself to run its business and websites. Spare capacity was created to allow Amazon to grow, and this now gives the opportunity for other businesses to use this spare capacity for themselves.

The key to consistent results is automation. Have servers build themselves from code and configuration that you and your team specify. This is where the developer world has had the biggest impact on the infrastructure and operations world.

Imagine clicking one button (or less if you schedule it) to build a complete application environment – from nothing to a complete server farm ready to serve your application. Depending on the size and complexity of your application, this could be from ten minutes to two hours. Putting together a few tools that work together can achieve this for you and your company.

Building servers

Server builds should be automated, as this enables easy creation of ready for work servers. They rely on some infrastructure and data to enable this.

- Operating System (OS) images
- Packages to Install, including dependencies and Docker images
- Configuration of the server and applications, usually kept in version control

- Network infrastructure (this too can be created by automation)
- Scheduler (to trigger actions based on time or other inputs)
- Certificate Authority (to enable Private Key Interchange for secure inter-server connections)
- Identity management (to control who has access to the server)
- Data and network connections as required
- Service Discovery or Domain Name Service (so the client can find the service to connect to)

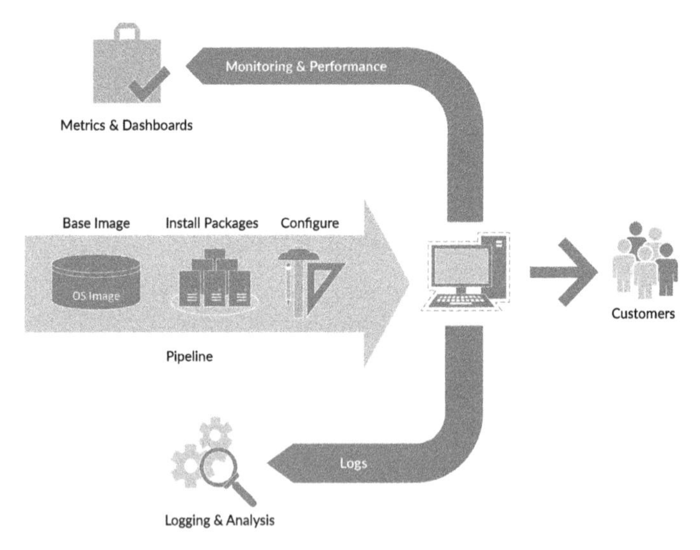

Figure 7.1: *Immutable server builds*

Ordering servers from internal virtualisation or external cloud providers means for every order, someone or something needs to build and configure that server for it to be useful and effective.

It's at this point that the capacity of the server needs to be decided. If the server is part of a software deployment, the architect may already have scoped and specified the size and number of servers required. This answers questions like: How fast and how many CPUs? How much memory? How much hard disk storage?

Virtual servers allow the choices to be easily changed later when more evidence related to real-time running of the server is known. The servers can be upgraded or even downgraded as the load changes dynamically.

Creation and management of these servers is achieved through a web interface. VMWare has VSphere, and the main cloud providers AWS, Azure and GCP have powerful web consoles.

You could do it this way, but it's not very automated or easily repeatable. Infrastructure as Code does cover this aspect too. Some companies may have their own tool for managing servers through the API, but due to different implementations, this might lock you into a cloud vendor, giving someone a lot of technical debt in refactoring code to work with a new vendor, should that choice be needed.

An alternative is to use a service like RightScale™, where they provide a web console and an API to manage servers, leaving their systems to deal with the complexity and differences between cloud providers. However, this could be another vendor lock in.

Fortunately, an open source tool called Terraform has this functionality programmed into it. Each cloud provider is a module within the code, allowing for slight differences between them, but due to the shared nature of servers, the same components exist and just might be called something different. Those differences are contained with configuration. With the flexible nature of Terraform and its modular approach to configuration, the differences can be minimised, relaxing the cloud vendor lock in issue.

If the configuration is designed with variables and modules, the variables holding the important stuff like server names, roles, size, etc, and the modules holding the cloud provider's specific nomenclature, swapping a module out will effectively swap the vendor. There would be a small number of other changes required, such as the back-end configuration (this is a state information cache for Terraform, so it can keep track of what it has done to eliminate duplication of effort), but it's less than if a custom tool was created.

With the physical provisioning of the server being provided for us, that leaves the following stages:

Bootstrap and base image

Any computer needs instructions to know what to do – the cloud is no exception. Rather than starting from a blank disk, cloud vendors provide base images to boot your new server from. These can vary wildly in functionality, from the basic operating system install to fully loaded software packages. The option to create your own also exists.

Like any software, these images need to be created and kept up to date. Of course, there are automated tools to do this, like Packer (www.packer.io), where a directory of files including a configuration file is loaded and an image is created from the results.

There is a trade-off between how much software is baked into the image and how often the image needs to be updated. The more software that is contained within the image, the more likely it is that one or more of those software packages will need an update. If it's automated, then the cost isn't more than a little more disk space, and some downtime (if any) to update the servers that were booted with that older image. If your servers are being destroyed every day, then there is no downtime.

Install packages

Additional software is required to run after boot. A template is used for virtual servers and further required software is installed. Depending on how much is baked into the boot image, this step may be merged with configuration.

At this point common software is installed if it's not included in the boot image, such as tools for source control, operations utilities including trusted root certificates, and other general use programs like Python, Ruby, etc that will help all steps from here on out in your organisation.

This stage includes the roles that the server is going to perform. If it's to be a DNS, then Bind might be installed. A web server, then Tomcat or Nginx.

Usually roles must be configured to work correctly, and this information may rely on private or internal artefacts (bundles of code), secrets (passwords and other sensitive information not stored in source control), and perhaps private repositories for custom tools. This shared configuration is usually done before the main application is installed and configured.

Configure

During this stage, the required settings are supplied so the installed software can operate.

Configuration management is used for installing and configuring software for consistent results. The main software is installed and configured so building the server is part of the software deployment steps.

Puppet and Chef (Chef is a fork of Puppet) are configuration management tools. They enable you to specify how you want your server built and configured through settings and shared modules, then they do the rest.

This configuration management isn't a one hit wonder though. The configuration can and should evolve with your environments and be updated as often as required for bug fixes and security updates.

Serve

The server is now ready to perform its purpose. It should take less than ten minutes to get to this stage from boot. Tools like Docker can reduce this by reducing the install and configure steps by deferring the building of containers to another process, leaving the server to just download them. Docker does this by baking everything into the image, so the boot time can be reduced to a time measured in seconds.

Monitor

Once the deployment steps are complete, a quick verification of the service by a task called a smoke test, alerts the rest of the infrastructure the server is ready. This might mean adding the server to a dynamic load balancer.

As the server performs its role, it will be subject to CPU, memory and disk usage. These as a minimum are monitored and the metrics are stored for later diagnostic use, and for the measuring and reporting of alarms. These alarms are set up to watch for scenarios such as high CPU usage over a period of minutes. This can happen at peak usage, and with the correct configuration, more servers can be quickly added to the cluster to serve that demand. It's usual to have a low CPU alarm, and this indicates when there are more servers than required by the users thus enabling the cluster to be scaled in and reducing the number of servers in the cluster.

Many metrics and statistics should be gathered and stored from the server in the event of a bug or other error. Having this data will help the engineers diagnosing the issue, and give them the opportunity to further improve the system.

The most popular open source monitoring stacks are made up of tools consisting of three parts:

- **Monitoring/Alerting:** Sensu is an open source tool that runs scheduled tasks against your servers called checks. With a wide range of plugins, this tool written in Ruby collects metrics and statistics from your servers. Uchiwa is an alerts dashboard working with Sensu, where it displays the status of the agents and servers, giving the option of raising alerts if any of the checks indicates an issue.

- **Logging:** The ELK or Elastic stack consists of a group of tools including Elasticsearch to store data, Logstash to interpret logs from the servers, and Kibana for visualising and searching through the logs.

- **Graphing or visualisation:** Once the data and logs are gathered, there is nothing like seeing a dashboard or graph on the screen. Grafana enables beautiful graphs of performance point series data to be displayed as a graph, together with threshold highlights. In addition, Smashing is very flexible for displaying statuses of servers, services, and even pipeline information if connected to a CI server like Jenkins.

This allows for the classic method of monitoring a server or service. USE, created by Brendan Gregg,[5] treats this information as a group of buckets of information.

---

5 www.brendangregg.com/usemethod.html

- **Utilisation (U):** The percentage of time a resource is in use
- **Saturation (S):** The amount of work the resource must complete but cannot service (the queue of work)
- **Errors (E):** A count of errors

This makes it easy to create graphs of how busy or utilised each part of an infrastructure is and how many errors it's creating. This is great for judging how busy a server is, but doesn't tell you anything about the applications or services running on that server.

As an alternative to USE, application user experience-based monitoring, Tom Wilkie developed a system focused on application performance called RED.[6]

- **Rate (R):** The number of requests per second
- **Errors (E):** The number of failed requests
- **Duration (D):** The amount of time to process a request

6 www.slideshare.net/weaveworks/monitoring-microservices

These metrics record how well the microservice is actually performing requests and reflects the user experience more closely.

Both approaches are important as they measure different things. USE provides infrastructure feedback (is the server big enough, is there enough memory), and RED is useful for developer feedback, to improve the performance of the service if it's developed in-house.

Prometheus is a great monitoring tool for capturing these from applications alongside or instead of Sensu.

By using instantly available virtual servers and automating the above steps, lead times also tumble from weeks to days to minutes.

When building servers, I have a few principles to guide me:

Immutable server: Once a server is built, its software, configuration and operating state never changes. This doesn't include data on the server, database files and documents. These are important and need their own processes and management. Any updating of software or configuration means a new server is built and the old one discarded, often through a blue-green pipeline. In this way, the configuration is stored in a version-controlled repository such as Git and allows for a known good configuration at any time.

Immutable server pattern: Most server workloads can lend themselves to temporary or elastic capacity. For example, your website might be busy in the afternoons, so more capacity is required than at night time when your customers are asleep. Temporary servers are provisioned, built and configured when the demand calls for them, and then are shut down and destroyed when no longer required.

You should design your server to make use of disposable components for every part of your application infrastructure that isn't the data. This means that once the server is built there are no further changes to the configuration or software. This gives the advantage of knowing exactly what the server will look like with every build, until the configuration is changed on purpose and the server rebuilt.

This means that any deployment scripts will run the same on every server based on that configuration build. With the building of each server, a certain baseline or base image will be used. AMIs provided by Amazon give a usable installation of the OS, upon which the configuration code and build can run.

This makes the deployment easier. However, from a security point of view, can lead to stale or out of date packages in the image. When dealing with any sort of image, it was stable at the point it was created and tested, but bugs and security issues are reported and fixed all the time, making that image a potential security target for hackers. Source control systems such as Git, together with a versioning scheme, will allow management of many packages, detailing what the changes or updates to each package are, as well as dates and other information to make it simple to see what each package does, when it changed, why it changed and when.

You must have a configuration management system that copes with or can track baked in features, with a procedure to either accept the risk, or keep the images refreshed.

Immutable infrastructure isn't a new thing. It was mentioned by O'Reilly in a blog post a few years ago.[7] There was a time when uptime was the key metric to a stable server. This was back in the days when hardware

7 www.oreilly.com/ideas/an-introduction-to-immutable-infrastructure

failures could take your server offline, or software updates would mean a reboot is needed. Working in the cloud requires a different metric: recovery time. This is the time it takes from something breaking or going wrong to the service being restored again.

When a new update was made available for deployment, a maintenance window was created where the users could expect the service to be unavailable. Engineers would then install and deploy the updated software within this window, often at unsociable hours, to cause minimal disruption to the customers.

But what if you have a server that can build itself from scratch? Or to spread the idea a little wider, a multi-server, multi-tier service and infrastructure from scratch? Building servers from scratch gives you deployment options. AWS provides auto scaling groups. I will cover these shortly. However, they do rely on having a server that can either build itself or one that is using a fully baked image.

The immutable model means that your server needs to be rebuilt to receive the updated configuration. In development environments, where the server is rebuilt from scratch every day, this isn't an issue, but in the production environment it may need a regular maintenance schedule, or a deployment roll-out if the architecture of the environment involves clusters or blue-green deployment to update and reduce downtime.

A blue-green deployment is where new or green servers are provisioned based on updated configuration, while leaving the current or blue servers in place. Once the provisioning or smoke tests have passed, marking the new servers as ready and usable, a mechanism – usually the load balancer for that service – is updated to serve requests from the new green servers. The old blue servers can then be decommissioned and destroyed. This process done correctly is seamless to the users of the service.

Docker and containers have gained popularity as a way of deploying software quickly. It's precisely due to their immutable nature that this works. A Docker container is a small version of a server. It contains all the software together with dependencies for the service to work, wrapped up in an image, ready to run. They can be created and destroyed in seconds.

Having this ability to create and destroy servers quickly and easily means you could also take advantage of billing choices where excess computing capacity at the cloud provider is auctioned cheaper. AWS call this

SPOT pricing, and in conjunction with immutable servers and auto scaling groups, can save you a lot of money over a large, static, long-running server deployment.

On-demand: Servers are only provisioned when they are required. The ability to build a server at any time, coupled with the pay-as-you-use cloud service, allows us to build a server when we need it and destroy it when it's no longer required.

Known state: Building from scratch or a minimal base image means, with the addition of software bundles, I have all the tools available to create a brand-new server in a known state of software and configuration at any time.

In the talk that I delivered at Puppet Camp London in 2017, I described how you can create Puppet code to build your servers independently from Puppet infrastructure (Masterless). In this way, each server can be created on its own, and you know what that server is going to look like and perform. Details of the talk can be found on my blog at www.neilmillard.com/blog.

Data: The architecture of the system allows for failures at any time. This means any data on the server is replicated and has a backup. Data is the only moving part in the system and therefore is the most delicate. Data integrity is key in any of my designs and is usually the reason for the server to exist. Careful management of data will minimise data loss. It's difficult to achieve all three of integrity, speed and availability, but with collaborative design, the trade-offs can be calculated and requirements can be met.

CASE STUDY: VERTICA SOFTWARE UPDATE WITH CONFIGURATION MANAGEMENT

The immutable model is fine for most applications, but when you have data to consider it adds an extra layer of complexity. In the case of a database server, keep the information safe while updating the software version, as well as any schema updates in the configuration the database needs, so the next time the server is built it is fully upgraded. Modifying the data could cause delays and data corruption. This is due to the old data being updated by the new software at install.

A blue-green deployment could work here, but as a database deals with data, you probably don't want two copies running simultaneously. What is needed is a more controlled approach.

For MoneySuperMarket, a blue-yellow-green deployment was chosen and deployed.

This follows the blue-green update, but with an intermediate step. The new yellow servers are built, the database is copied and kept synchronised with the blue servers. With an agreed data freeze window of about thirty to forty-five minutes (depending on the speed of the following steps), the yellow servers are then upgraded by an automated task, checked for data consistency, and then shut down to make the attached data volumes or disks available. At this point the blue-green process continues as outlined above, with the new green servers using the updated disk volumes that have been prepared by the yellow servers. Once green builds, the service is updated and new requests flow to the green servers. The data freeze is then melted, enabling the old blue servers to be switched off, then ultimately deleted or decommissioned once the integrity of the new data is okay and no rollback is required.

EIGHT

Scaling Infrastructure and Applications

Dealing with spikes and lulls in demand requires careful consideration in order for the application to still function at its best. Automatically scaling groups is the ability first introduced by AWS to use monitoring metrics to decide automatically to increase or decrease the number of nodes in a cluster. Configuration for this is provided, such as the server image, server type, and how long to wait before the next step up or down can occur. In addition, a node minimum and maximum number is also required.

The cluster will be monitored, and using the rules specified in the configuration, will grow or shrink the number of cluster nodes as required. A server can only deal with a specific load before it reaches its own limitations and bottlenecks.

To overcome these limits, more memory, disk or compute (CPU) is added to the application. This can be done in one of two ways: increasing the size of components inside a server (scaling up), or increasing the number of servers able to handle the requests in a load balancing cluster (scaling out).

Scaling up

The difficulty of upgrading an existing server shares many traits with creating a new server in the first place, like ordering and lead time for the components and setup time before the server can be used again. In a physical environment, the application will be running badly while you wait for the new components to be ordered and delivered.

Once that wait is over, scheduling of the downtime can now commence. The server will be switched off and unavailable for use while the upgrade occurs. If the server should fall into the delicate category, there can be huge risks with turning it off and hoping it can start again without major incident.

Scaling out

Instead of the risks associated with scaling up, the service could be scaled out and you can take advantage of multiple servers. This will require a certain amount of work around the application design and configuration to enable.

For instance, you will need a load balancer, and to make sure the application can work with multiple servers. This can either be in a true load-balanced manner, spreading the load and users among all the available servers, or sometimes it's necessary to use sticky sessions, where the user stays on the first server they hit for the remainder of their session. This does risk the user losing their session or some work if that specific server fails mid-session. Scaling this process up into a whole environment is easy when tackled one server at a time.

Scaling in

Anyone can spin up a server: the challenge is terminating the older servers when the demand is no longer required.

It should be obvious that you don't want to terminate a server while it's in use. Some software already exists to assist in this. For instance, the EC2 plugin for Jenkins will both create new slaves (servers that help do the work with the Jenkins master) when there is insufficient capacity to run jobs, as well as terminate old ones when there are no jobs to run on any given server.

Load balancers are capable of draining a server in preparation for it to be terminated. This is easier to do when using a blue-green deployment, where a group of servers is no longer accepting new connections. A monitor task simply checks if the connections on a server are closed before marking the server as redundant.

Your application or DevOps team will need to come up with a way to scale in without service interruption, and will need a robust level of design to get it right.

Application load balancing

As the application is no longer tied to a single massive server, why not have two smaller ones, and balance the load between them? With this design in mind, this gives massive wins to leverage cloud features like auto scaling, and gives the option of choosing the best size and cost of server for the load experienced.

This is how sites like Wikipedia can scale to serve the whole world with their content, allowing thousands of people to view and edit pages at a time. Every tier of the application can run on an independent server and share the load with its team within the load balance group.

Application auto scaling

Auto scaling greatly reduces upfront costs, and with the flexibility of cloud compute resource, can enable gradual increase in capacity to serve the application with its micro service.

Scaling the application from the smallest service to many servers in a load balance group allows the service to remain online to all consumers while at the same time reducing its cost footprint to you when it isn't required. Auto scaling can be controlled and triggered from a couple of sources.

- **Scheduling based on the time of day:** If you know your services are going to be busy at specific times of day or week, the schedule can be configured to activate more or less servers based around these times.
- **Compute or CPU usage:** With monitoring in place, triggers can be set up so that if certain thresholds are passed, either on the way up (busy) or down (quieter), the appropriate number of servers can be made available.
- **Memory usage:** Any metric that is being monitored can be used as a threshold trigger, so if this application uses a lot of memory and that is a better indication of load than CPU, this metric can be used instead or in addition to others.

Putting these concepts together will result in a scalable application, with the infrastructure to go with it. In addition, the Key Performance Indicator is no longer uptime (the length of time a server has been operating since the last power on or reboot), but recovery time – the time it takes from outage to full recovery and serving customers again.

Provision scripts in Bash or Ruby then prepare the server by downloading the source and configuration and tools to build the server. Ansible, Chef or Puppet then act on the configuration, resulting in a server ready to work for you.

I would then ensure the server is ready by checking the monitoring stats from your pipeline before the code then adds it into an operation state via a load balancer or DNS entry, ready for the users to access it.

The second part of automation is ensuring the monitoring continues to report the server status after it has been built, to ensure smooth operation and to alert staff to any potential issues.

I would write further code to run in case of a failure, like I said, things do fail. During the architecture step, single points of failure are identified and will be addressed by code and monitoring. This enables the server to recover itself when these error conditions exist. For instance, in a database cluster, I have code that will check the status of the cluster that node is about to become part of during the provisioning process.

If the cluster is operational during the build step, then the previous server must have crashed or become otherwise unavailable (switched off for example) and the node should execute the node recovery code, synchronise data, and join the existing cluster, rather than the normal provisioning procedure.

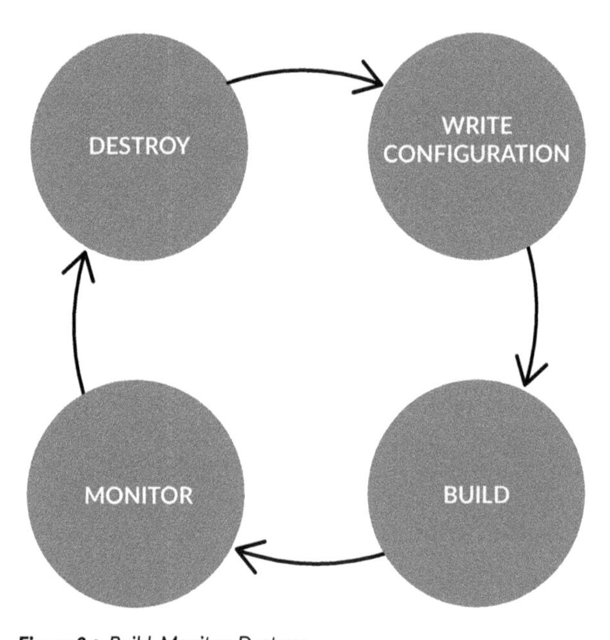

***Figure 8.1**: Build, Monitor, Destroy*

With this code in place, the cluster could lose a server node and build a new one automatically, reducing risk and downtime. I have done this for HP Vertica and MongoDB database clusters without losing any data.

The third part of the automation is shutting down and cleaning up. For test environments, it would be reasonable to destroy and not pay for them overnight. Because I am confident the code and configuration can build the server from scratch with very little intervention, having a schedule to build it ready for the working day following its destruction in the evening gives me the choice to not run the server overnight.

Shutting the servers down in a controlled and clean way is preferred, especially if we are looking to retain certain data. A backup should be taken that the server can recover from in the morning, before the code destroys the server.

NINE

Cost Control

Controlling your costs is an important aspect of any business and project – with cloud projects this is even more important due to the number of decisions that can have a drastic effect on your monthly AWS bill.

The four main areas that will affect your costs are unused or forgotten resources, AWS application design, correct sizing of resources, and discount options such as reserved instances.

Unused resources

Your ongoing battle is going to be with resources that have been created and used for a short while, then left running or allocated to your account. With the ease of creating resources and human nature, unless managed these resources can be left and forgotten until someone spots it on the itemised AWS bill.

Fortunately, there are a number of tools you can use to help keep this spend under control. On the billing dashboard of your account, along with a summary and bill information, you can activate Cost Explorer, a tool to explore the current costs incurred on your account.

For offline analysis, reports are available to a selection of AWS services called Cost Allocation Tags. These enable your team to tag a resource for the purposes of tracking costs. You could use a purchase order or project code or name to show up in the reports.

In addition to these tools, you're also able to create alarms via CloudWatch, to alert you when a billing threshold has been breached.

Resources most commonly forgotten are EC2 instances, Elastic IP addresses that are no longer attached to an instance, unattached EBS volumes, snapshots and RDS instances.

AWS application design

An important aspect of any workload or application you run or plan to run on cloud services is the design of the application and the infrastructure it runs on. This is due to the balance between performance, availability and cost. Let me demonstrate with two examples.

EC2 vs. Lambda

Is your microservice designed to run with Lambda? This is where your code is designed to run without provisioning or managing servers and executes only when needed and scales based on demand from a few requests per day to thousands per second.

If your code is written in one of the computer languages that Lambda supports (Node.js, Java, C# or Python), Lambda might be a good choice. All the power and flexibility without the need to manage the infrastructure and servers.

The infrastructure you already have may affect your choice and so EC2 might be best. How do you decide?

Like many of AWS's services, they build the Lambda service on top of the components available to any of their customers, like EC2 or Elastic Container Service. They manage the infrastructure so this attracts the management costs as part of your bill.

This billing model can work for or against you depending on the utilisation of the service. If you expect a high utilisation level, and have the support staff to look after the infrastructure, it's usually better value to host the service on EC2 instances that your team can provision, configure and maintain.

The precise level varies per service and a break-even chart can be created.

EC2 requests per hour	*AWS Lambda Container Function*
295,000	100 ms execution with 128MB
64,000	200 ms execution with 512MB

In the table, I've broken down the number of requests per hour running on an EC2 m4.medium instance similar to the Lambda container specification and function execution time so that each line has an equal cost.

Performance testing of your application's microservice and typical workload are needed so you know how many requests running on an EC2 instance would provide adequate performance.

EC2 instances availability is nine to five or twenty-four-seven. You only pay for what you use – so how about no servers running at all?

Many environments exist purely for developers and as such don't see any activity outside of regular business hours. With the appropriate level of provisioning automation, whole environments can be switched on fresh in the morning before the teams get ready to work, and decommissioned in the evening after a day's work.

In a week, there are 168 hours. In a nine-to-five work week, there are only forty hours. That is less than 25% of the time. If you only run the servers when you need them, you can save 75% of the cost of running them twenty-four-seven!

One of my clients required at least one server to always be available, and scaled the service to a ready workload at 7am and scaled back at 9pm. During the day, the CPU and memory are monitored and if specific thresholds are met, the server application increased or decreased the number of online servers in the cluster. Not only did this help increase availability for busy periods of the day, it still provided substantial savings over running a static server farm.

Another way to reduce the need for expensive processing servers is to cache the results and output to edge servers. These servers don't require the processing power of the main application and therefore are cheaper to run.

These cheaper front-end servers handle many of the requests, leaving the expensive (in terms of compute) jobs to the back-end application servers. Delegating the easy content to the edge servers means you require less expensive application servers, so you save money and increase response times to your users.

Server instance sizing

When migrating a service, you don't have to have the same size server (in terms of compute and memory), which enables more appropriate sizing of the server to be deployed, depending on the workload. As mentioned above, workloads can be different between the front-end and back-end servers, and based on scaling and workload, can enable optimisation of the application performance as well as costs.

Often a greater number of smaller servers (rather than a few larger servers) gives you the flexibility to follow the workload closely. Of course, if the demand is relatively static, that may suit your application better.

This is where monitoring can show dividends regarding the utilisation of resources such as server CPU and memory, allowing intelligent decisions to be made.

Reserved resources

AWS provides further billing options to reduce your costs. If you know roughly what your demand for resources is going to be, you can opt to pre-order vouchers to be used against charges for various AWS resources that will discount the monthly bill in exchange for an upfront commitment for one to three years.

Summary

Following the four steps will help migrate or build your applications in the cloud.

1. Design the application cloud.
2. Automate the infrastructure.
3. Scale for flexible workloads.
4. Keep the data safe.

For more information, visit my website, www.neilmillard.com, where you will find information, blogs and speaking appearances.

APPENDIX

Key Concepts

Information Technology (IT) has many terms that you may or may not be familiar with. I will cover a few here that you can probably skip over if you're not new to servers and cloud technologies.

Amazon Web Services – AWS

Public cloud provider. Created out of necessity, AWS is the infrastructure that Amazon itself uses to run its business and websites. Spare capacity was created to allow Amazon to grow, and this now gives the opportunity for other businesses to use this spare capacity for themselves.

Blockers

These are issues that the team have identified as halting or slowing down progress. They are often related to a broken or slow business process, or a policy decision that is beyond the control of the team.

Capital expense (CapEx)

The money a company spends to buy, maintain and improve its fixed assets, such as buildings, vehicles and hardware.

Computer process

A program that provides results (outputs) based on predefined rules (program) and data (inputs).

Inputs > program task > outputs

Configuration management

Puppet, Chef or Ansible is installed as part of the boot image and used to provision the software on the server itself. This is a key part of the server provisioning and build process, as this is the chunk of Infrastructure as Code that defines the server role and gives it tasks to play in your environment.

Chef and Puppet both have their roots in a tool called CFEngine. This means they share many key ideas and are both written in Ruby. They also come from the point of view that if the infrastructure as code defines a desired state, then the program works, sometimes as a series of simultaneous tasks, to make that end state on the server.

Ansible has different roots and is written in Python. The approach here is much closer to scripting, where the code describes what should happen and which order it should work through the instructions.

Containers

A subset of **virtualisation**, where a virtual server can run instances of a program or service in an isolated jail.

Continuous integration

With the tests and code available in code repositories, continuous integration allows the continuous running of the tests whenever a new piece of code is committed. This enables the feedback loop to be as short as possible and identify errors almost immediately. This in turn improves efficiency, as the bugs are fixed before the programming moves onto another task.

CPU

Central Processing Unit: provides the computer the power to run programs and tasks.

Data centre

A dedicated space that is climate-controlled and secure, for the housing and operation of servers. These usually restrict physical access to the servers, and have may redundant systems to ensure continuous running.

Dependencies

To save time and effort, open source code can use existing programs and libraries. These dependencies need to be installed alongside the developers' code for the application to work.

Hybrid private and public cloud

Many businesses already have data centres of their own and run virtual workloads with technology from VMWare, Citrix Xen and Hyper-V. Private cloud refers to the ability of internal staff to order on-demand, virtual servers, without the direct intervention of IT or using an external public cloud.

Hypervisor

A system that runs virtual machines on a hardware server. The three leaders are Xen by Citrix, VMWare and Microsoft's Hyper-V.

Infrastructure

The provision of all the components of the computer ecosystem. Storage, memory, CPU and networking that run the services to be consumed.

Infrastructure as Code (IaC)

A new concept that has arisen through the widespread use of virtual machine sprawl blended with software programming techniques to manage the building of servers, and control of the now virtualised network equipment that provides the connections in between.

Infrastructure as a Service (IaaS)

The provisioning of Infrastructure via cloud services.

Kanban

Kanban is an inventory and scheduling system. Its use in software development is like SCRUM; however, the tasks are not timeboxed but subject to other measures and limits, like waiting task queue lengths, with emphasis on throughput, through control of new tasks coming into the queue and reducing defects.

Memory

A temporary store of data.

- **Non-Volatile:** Memory that is able to retain data for long periods of time, like tape, disks, and CD-ROMs

- **RAM:** Random access memory, can read and write
- **ROM:** Read-only memory

Network

A direct or indirect connection between computers. A computer network enables the sharing of data between computers. Early examples used modems to connect over phone lines. This enabled the early email systems to deliver mail. In offices, computers are often linked using direct cables to a central point, enabling point to point communications between any connected computers. The central point often being interconnected Network Switches.

Operational expenses (OpEx)

The ongoing cost for running a product, business or system.

Pair programming

Often tasks can be complete faster and more effectively when people work in pairs. The best example is that of making two flat-packed wardrobes. You could give the task of assembling the wardrobes to two people acting on one wardrobe each. They would no doubt complete the task; however, you can probably see the benefits of the two people working together to make one wardrobe, then the other.

Pipeline

A defined process, usually on a continuous integration server, that automates the building, testing and deployment of code to the infrastructure, so that it delivers value to the product.

Rack

A specialised cabinet to house servers, network switches and computer hardware, providing power and sufficient airflow for cooling.

SCRUM

A framework for organising tasks with an emphasis on software development. This is where teams of three to nine work on given tasks in a timeboxed period known as a sprint.

Server

A computer that is connected to the network for the purpose of sharing access to processes or data stored on it. Examples include file servers for sharing files, Web servers for serving web pages accessed by a web browser, and gaming servers for a central point for coordinating online games.

Source control

A key part of iterative development is the storing of code, including application, service and infrastructure, within a history and version-controlled repository. This enables any team member to see what changed and when, as well as being a useful view in terms of auditing. Source control can also help when tracking down defects introduced during the development process.

Test-driven development

This is the programming practice where the test code is written first. A test simply ensures that given the specified input to a process or function, the given output is correctly produced.

The function or process is then created and checked against the test. This approach means that during the entire lifecycle of the process or function, you know the state of the tests and have ensured that new functionality can be added without breaking the current working state.

Virtualisation

Due to the advances in CPU and the capacity of computers, to improve efficiency and utilisation of hardware (physical computers) virtualisation is a way of running more than two logical computers in an isolated way (they are not aware they are sharing) on the same physical computer, and therefore share some of the capacity of that machine. This provides cost savings through better utilisation of hardware, space, cooling and other physical requirements, while delivering the same level of results from the virtual servers. The hypervisor mediates access to the hardware resources.

The Author

Neil Millard is a successful business entrepreneur, speaker and trainer, passionate about personal development and education.

Neil is well known as a techie when it comes to cloud and automated server infrastructures. He assists businesses in embracing new technology such as the cloud to move faster, become more automated and respond to customers' wants and needs.

Having spent many years in the financial sector with clients such as Barclays, Lloyds and AXA, he is now on a mission to share his wide sphere of financial knowledge with the world. Neil has seen all sides of the personal and business financial spectrum – from bankruptcy to business ownership – working with enterprise servers for blue chip companies for more than twenty years, and managing them within virtual private clouds and public cloud environments.

Recognised with Microsoft, HP and ITIL accreditations, Neil has used his knowledge and experience to tame manual deployments and upgrade methods, automate monitoring and scaling applications, and deploy on-demand Cloud Infrastructure as Code platforms. He has also spoken at IT events such as the prestigious Puppet Camp about dynamic cloud-based applications using the latest technologies, including Puppet and Docker.

Neil has delivered continuous integration projects like the blue-yellow-green upgrade of HP Vertica in Amazon Web Services. Neil worked to ensure this database system used for Artificial Intelligence required minimal downtime (about fifteen minutes) to enable MoneySuperMarket to seamlessly upgrade the database version without any data loss and deliver even more value to their clients.

If your business is ready to embrace the fast-paced world of cloud and be a fellow pioneer in the industry – or you've already taken some steps – Neil will guide you through the common pitfalls and lead you and your business to the agile and stable platform to scale with ease.

Find out more here:

www.neilmillard.com
Neil Millard
neil_millard

Lightning Source UK Ltd.
Milton Keynes UK
UKHW022047250119
336071UK00013B/577/P